Ask
BEARDERS

Ask
BEARDERS

Answers
to the
World's Most
Challenging
Cricket Questions

Bill Frindall

1 3 5 7 9 10 8 6 4 2

Published in 2009 by BBC Books,
an imprint of Ebury Publishing.
A Random House Group Company

The Random House Group Limited Reg. No. 954009

Addresses for companies within the Random House Group can
be found at
www.randomhouse.co.uk

A CIP catalogue record for this book is available from the British
Library.

ISBN 978 1 84607 880 4

The Random House Group Limited supports The Forest
Stewardship Council (FSC), the leading international forest
certification organisation. All our titles that are printed on
Greenpeace approved FSC certified paper carry the FSC logo.
Our paper procurement policy can be found at
www.rbooks.co.uk/environment

Commissioning editor: Albert DePetrillo
Editor: Nick Constable
Project editors: Steve Tribe and Kari Speers
Production: Antony Heller

Printed and bound in the UK by CPI Mackays, Chatham ME5 8TD

To buy books by your favourite authors and register for offers,
visit www.rbooks.co.uk

Contents

Foreword

This delightful book was not intended to be a tribute to Bill Frindall's life – merely to his work. The fact is, however, that Bill's character and humour leaps out at you from every page and from each of his replies to the sorts of questions that I tormented him with for 18 years. Mind you, I was not always guaranteed to receive an answer, apart from some muttering deep into his beard and a deliberately fixed focus on the cricket straight ahead!

Testing Bill's vast memory and quite staggering capacity to research even the most apparently mundane statistic was one of my most enjoyable pastimes on *Test Match Special*. Some questions might be purely mischievous – when the passage of play was dull, perhaps – but usually it was a serious enquiry brought about by the fascination of every aspect of this wonderful game that we all share. Bill's particular love, of course, was statistics – something that never gripped me in quite the same way even when I was playing. But like many of our listeners, I found myself increasingly interested in cricket's facts and figures because of Bill's natural ability to present them entertainingly and give them context. Indeed, Bill's greatest skill was to put fun into the apparently mundane role of scoring.

Brian Johnston christened him 'the Bearded Wonder' because Bill was able to produce answers to the commentators' questions even while he was scoring a test match in the minutest detail. Bill's good-natured nemesis, Steve Pittard from Huish Episcopi, is often first off the mark with the correct answer via email, but Bill's primary role, after all, was to produce a record so precise and detailed that he could tell me, hours later, to which part of the ground Kevin Pietersen's third four of the day was struck. This was due to his scoring system – a bewildering mass of squiggles and hieroglyphics that I never understood after all these years – which was the real reason for Bill's notoriety as a statistician, and the fascination of the listeners in him.

Visitors to the *Test Match Special* commentary box had one thing in common in that they all wanted to watch Bill in action. Sitting at the front table surrounded apparently chaotically by watches, sheets of paper, pens of different colour and type, at least one laptop and a mountain of files, Bill commanded a corner. It really was his territory and woe betide any unfortunate commentator who trespassed into it – even when hosting a crowded on-air discussion during an interval when Bill was not actually in the box! His return would be accompanied by a series of snorts and harrumphs and, if that did not do the trick, one's chair would then receive a firm shove in the back regardless of whether you were actually talking at the time or not. Visitors, however, were always welcomed very warmly into Bill's corner, and many of our celebrity guests taking *A View from the Boundary* on Saturday lunchtime would spend much of the day sitting alongside Bill.

It is clear that we have lost much more than merely a great scorer. Bill really was the cornerstone of *Test Match Special* and one of the true characters of our quirky soap opera. To work alongside him was a great privilege as well as enormous fun, and just as top cricketers provide inspiration for future generations, one glance at this collection of questions from his loyal listeners all over the world demonstrates the legacy of Bill Frindall – without doubt, cricket's finest statistician.

Jonathan Agnew

Introduction

The inevitable problem with this snapshot of Bill Frindall's vast cricketing knowledge is that – were he still alive – he'd have done the thing so much better. As a prolific cricket writer and broadcaster, his attention to detail, command of statistics and fierce enthusiasm for the craft of scoring were legendary within the game. Given the task of editing this book, he would have had a hundred entries selected, indexed and cross-referenced by lunch on the first day. Sadly, fate robbed us of one of cricket's great characters on 30 January 2009 and, for the first time in 246 home tests – an Ashes year to boot – listeners to the BBC's *Test Match Special* are without the voice of the 'Bearded Wonder'. For two, perhaps three, generations of fans, English summers can never be the same again.

This is not a book about Bill's personal story – his own autobiography, *Bearders: My Life in Cricket*, is the place for that. Suffice to say that his vital career statistics are as follows. He was born William Howard Frindall in Epsom, Surrey, on 3 March 1939 – the first day of the famous South Africa-England 'Timeless Test' (which lasted so long the English tourists were in danger of missing their boat home). After leaving Reigate Grammar School, he studied architecture before a spell of national service led to what he later described as 'six-and-a-half seasons for the RAF'. Throughout this period he played club cricket wherever and whenever he could; bowling fast and, as one commentator would later laconically observe, 'optimistically'.

His big break came in 1965 when, noting the death of the first *TMS* scorer Arthur Wrigley, he wrote to the BBC applying for the job. Duly appointed, he scored his first Test match at Old Trafford on 2 June 1966 (when England entertained the West Indies) and never missed a home Test thereafter. Throughout his BBC career he relished any opportunity to explain how he got started and would solemnly advise would-be scorers to 'keep an eye on the obituary columns'.

Black humour was undoubtedly one of his great joys, but it was with genuine delight that he later advised Wrigley's son Steve about the value of Arthur's cricket memorabilia. After dispensing some sales tips, Bill recalled how he 'applied for [Arthur's] job and began the next summer on a three-match trial and was found not guilty!'

As the 1960s rolled on, so Frindall's broadcasting reputation grew, largely through banter with the likes of fellow commentators Brian Johnston and John Arlott. Later he played the curmudgeon to BBC cricket correspondent Jonathan Agnew, who would delight in teasing him about the state of his beard or occasional dogged stubbornness on cricketing terminology. With a guttural grunt, Frindall would verbally cuff his tormentors aside – sometimes tapping the window to remind them of the job in hand.

His BBC website blog began on 16 May 2001. It was titled 'Stump the Bearded Wonder' and invited cricket lovers to submit a question in the hope that he would be unable to answer. Few succeeded, although some of the more arcane queries – 'How many ambidextrous First-Class cricketers born in May scored less than 20 on their debut?' – got short shrift. (That question was made up by the way. As we'll see, it's sometimes hard to tell.)

Poor old Friarmere111 certainly got some chin music when he emailed observing that 'in the recent Yorkshire v Notts match … Yorkshire had 11 lbws against them. Is this a record number of lbws in a match?'

'It may be,' replied Bill (and you can almost hear the weary sigh). 'No one has scoured nearly 50,700 First-Class matches to find out!'

The blog later became known as 'Ask Bearders' and developed into a social networking site on the *TMS* homepage; a kind of virtual-anorak heaven in which contributors plumbed hitherto uncharted depths of cricket trivia. So we learn that Bob Crisp (Rhodesia, Western Province, Worcestershire and South Africa) is the only Test cricketer to climb Mount Kilimanjaro twice. We discover that England wicket-keeper Tommy Ward is not only the sole First-Class batsman to feature in two hat-tricks on the same day (Old Trafford v Australia, 1912) but is also the only Test cricketer to have been electrocuted in a gold mine. And – not one for the nervous, this – we are given incontrovertible proof that the great Sir Donald Bradman is a fibber: 'The Don did NOT score 1,000 First-Class runs IN MAY. Only three players have achieved that feat: W.G. Grace (Gloucestershire) in 1895, W.R. Hammond (Gloucestershire) in 1927, and C. Hallows (Lancashire) in 1928.'

There are also some irresistible Frindallisms, such as when Aaron of Newcastle upon Tyne imagines that Bill is 'not fond of all the new innovations' in modern limited-overs cricket. 'Yes,' agrees Bill, 'I have always favoured old innovations.' When William Boyle of Norfolk, England enquires as to how many Test wickets 'Beefy' got in his Test career, Bearders is clearly unimpressed. 'I assume,' he replies huffily, 'you are referring to Ian Botham.'

On several occasions he clearly suspects his *TMS* colleagues – particularly prank-addict David 'Bumble' Lloyd – of submitting questions about fictitious events in the hope of luring him into hours of research. Some (probably innocent) cricket lovers also find their questions hammered through the covers. When Baz Druker, England, asks Bearders: 'Who is the only England Test cricketer ever to have stood as a parliamentary candidate?' he is curtly informed: 'Another trick question? There have been at least two.'

Frindall finds his best form, however, when he gets

down and dirty on cricket trivia. Anyone who's not a cricket fan and doesn't follow *TMS* would be forgiven for regarding the next couple of paragraphs from 'Ask Bearders' as both baffling and completely bonkers:

Q While compiling statistics for Cleethorpes Cricket Club, our statistician found the instance of a Mr Lord, who collapsed and died of a heart attack whilst batting. The book recorded his departure "retired dead", and his career average had been calculated with this counted as being out. Is this correct, or should a batsman retiring injured, or indeed dead, be counted as not out for such purposes? **Michael Shelton**

BEARDERS' ANSWER: Unless a batsman retires bored, his departure should be recorded as 'retired not out'. This includes death and injury. It also includes compassionate retirements to visit seriously ill relatives or to accompany their pregnant wives to hospital ('retired to become a father'). Only voluntary retirements, when the batsman has no intention of resuming his innings, count as a wicket. All the others should be treated as 'not out' in calculating averages.

Finally, lest anyone think that scoring is one long joke, it's clear that certain issues touched a Frindall nerve. Take for instance this response to a query from Bipin Dani (India). Bipin was interested in Bill's view on the

International Cricket Council's decision to change the result of the notorious 2006 Oval Test between Pakistan and England from forfeiture to draw. 'I know this was the only "forfeited" Test in history,' writes Bipin, blithely, 'but are there any other instances when the other results of tests have been changed after so many days or months?'

'There is no precedent,' fumes Bearders, 'for the result of a Test match being changed after the day of its completion, and this latest in a lengthening list of contentious and politically motivated decisions by the ICC has set an extremely dangerous precedent.'

He concludes: 'Law 21 (10) states that "Once the umpires have agreed with the scorers the correctness of the scores at the conclusion of the match the result cannot thereafter be changed." In my records, and in those of many other statisticians, this result will remain as a forfeited victory to England.'

It's a measure of Bill Frindall's status among cricket lovers that when the game's future historians debate that Oval Test – and many hundreds of others – it'll be his scorecard that counts.

Nick Constable

Best of Bearders

(Q) Why is a cricket box called a 'box' when it clearly isn't? A box should be capable of being fully closed. **AMS, UK**

BEARDERS' ANSWER: According to the *Oxford English Reference Dictionary*, the word 'box' has 14 different meanings, none of which mentions 'capable of being fully closed'. No. 11 is 'a light shield for protecting the genitals in sport, esp. cricket.'

Perhaps the origins stem from Pandora's Box (of evils). A CASKET would surely be a better receptacle for Crown Jewels.

(Q) Am I right in remembering that Aggers [BBC Cricket Correspondent Jonathan Agnew] hit 76 v Yorks at Scarboro' in the 80s? I went home at the end of the first (rain affected) day and Aggers was at the crease.

When I arrived the next morning, unfortunately I

missed the first hour – delayed somehow on the 40-mile journey from Thirsk – I couldn't believe the scoreboard. Leics had scored about 150 in the first hour and Aggers was no longer at the crease but had apparently scored a whirlwind 76!

It was one of the most entertaining innings I never saw! **Paul Latham, England**

BEARDERS' ANSWER: No one in their right mind should remember anything about the batsmanship of Jon Agnew!

I must have scored his four Test innings (5 and 2 not out v West Indies and 1 no v Sri Lanka in 1984; 2 no v Australia in 1985), but happily all memory of those tail-end epics has been wiped clean.

The Scarborough innings was 90 (not 76) as nightwatchman in 1987 and remained his highest score. He could no doubt produce a 300-page thesis on it.

Wisden restricts its comments to: 'Agnew hit a spectacular, career-best 90 from 68 balls, including six sixes and eight fours, and then took the first five Yorkshire wickets to fall.'

The three-day match was drawn: Leics 365-8d and 188-8d; Yorks 265-9d and 184-5.

 My Dad, playing for a local village side, once took wickets with both of his last two balls of a season. He then missed the entire next season due to injury before returning a couple of months into the next season and taking a wicket with his first ball – completing a fairly long-winded hat-trick of sorts.

Do you know of any similarly long-winded hat-tricks or other bowling feats? **Rick De'Laglio**

BEARDERS' ANSWER: No, I do not. Your Dad's triple strike is probably unique. Of course, hat-tricks can only be claimed within the same match – not within the same lifetime! It would take a player with Geoffrey Boycott's supreme dedication to personal records to even notice that he had achieved such a feat.

Q Do you record a player's weight? If so, who (at their heaviest) was the heaviest person to play for England? Some contenders I can think of: Colin Milburn, Andrew Flintoff, Devon Malcolm, Robin Smith, Ian Botham, Graham Gooch and of course Mike Gatting. **RobM1974**

BEARDERS' ANSWER: Pity you've hidden your identity behind a code – is this yet another bizarre, newfangled fashion that has passed me by? I'm sure that the last six names on your list would enjoy meeting you on a dark night!

No, I don't keep a record of players' weights because they tend to vary season by season. W.G. Grace and

Alfred Mynn must be near the top of England's list of heavyweights. One of the heaviest Test cricketers was Australia's Warwick Armstrong, whose shirt used to occupy most of a wall of the museum at the MCG. Known as 'The Big Ship', he weighed 22 stone at the end of his First-Class playing career in February 1922.

Q A rather unusual incident occurred whilst playing a league game a few Sundays ago. We were playing on a little village green in Benenden with very short straight boundaries and our fast bowler was on. On one occasion he bowled a ball with a bit of extra pace and it flew past the batsman and burst through the keeper's gloves, hitting him on the head and going for six byes! I was wondering if there is any other instance of six byes being given in First-Class cricket or any other form of cricket you have records for. **Dan, Kent**

BEARDERS' ANSWER: Thank you Dan for revealing both your name and county – very refreshing!

It should have been signalled as four byes. You cannot score six of anything except for hits off the bat – see Law 19 (4.b).

My XI used to play an annual match at Benenden. Their sightscreens used to be stored in the adjacent vicarage during the winter months until a new incumbent, unfamiliar with cricket, grew his runner beans up them.

Q One of my ancestors is Bobby Peel, who played for Yorkshire and England but was (to put it bluntly) a drunk. He fell down the steps at either Headingley or Lord's and Lord Hawke kicked him out of Yorkshire and England cricket. Can you shed any light on him, his life and his (ahem) misdemeanours please?
Alison Bottomley

BEARDERS' ANSWER: Thank you, Alison, for one of the most fascinating questions I have received.

Bobby Peel (1857–1941) was the second of Yorkshire's outstanding left-arm spinners after Ted Peate. In a First-Class career of 436 matches between 1882 and 1899, he took 1,775 First-Class wickets at 16.20 runs apiece, scored 12,191 runs at 19.44, hit seven centuries and held 214 catches. In just 20 Test matches he took 101 wickets at 16.98.

An exceptionally thirsty man, Peel came on to the field at Bramall Lane, Sheffield, in August 1897 having lunched well. He might have got away with it if he hadn't urinated on the pitch in front of Lord Hawke, who promptly banished him from the Yorkshire XI. Peel did make four further First-Class appearances (for the South, the Players, A.J. Webbe's XI and, finally, for an England XI v the 1899 Australians at Truro). Years later, when his flannels had dried, Lord Hawke stated: 'He never bore me any malice.'

Q Hi Bill, I wonder if you remember touring Germany in the 1980s with the Pioneers and playing against an RAF Germany XI, for whom I was match manager, when a tractor pulling manure started to spread it over the outfield? It took us some time to explain to the local employee that we were actually playing a game of cricket. Have you seen any other humorous or unusual stopped-play incidents? **Flt Lt Bob Patrick (rtd), England**

BEARDERS' ANSWER: Good to hear from you again, Bob. Reinforced by West Indies and Hampshire stroke maker Roy Marshall, the touring Pioneers, still celebrating their win against Standard Athletic at Meudon, near Paris, played your XI at RAF Wildrenrath in September 1979. Your cunning ploy in enticing a maverick muck spreader's surprise attack on the outfield only narrowly failed to halt our victory march.

I have played in matches where horses or neighbouring bonfires invaded the playing area and a cow ate the only match ball. The first match my own XI played ended when the opposing captain, also aged 10, fell victim to an imaginative lbw decision and stormed off the ground with our only bat – his!

Q What is the highest number of runs a player has scored in Test matches without EVER being dismissed? **Ben, Italy**

BEARDERS' ANSWER: The answer is 66 by Afaq Hussain of Pakistan. He appeared in two Test matches, batting at number ten on three occasions and at nine once, scoring 10* and 35* v England at Lahore in October 1961 and 8* and 13* v Australia at Melbourne in December 1964. His off-spin was less successful, claiming a solitary wicket from 37 overs at a cost of 106 runs.

His name led to Brian Johnston playing his most famous prank on a hapless Rex Alston at Lord's during Pakistan's 1962 tour of England.

Q As a child, I was a great fan of the batting of Bob Willis. He looked so uncomfortable when he was batting and I know he never made 30 for England. However, I think he still holds a number of batting records for England in terms of not outs and batting partnerships.

Can you enlighten us Bill and also possibly explain why world-class attacks found him so difficult to get out?
Terry T, England

BEARDERS' ANSWER: Willis did hold the world Test record for most not outs with 55 from 128 innings but this was surpassed by Courtney Walsh with 61 from 185. His highest score was 28 not out.

He still shares in two tenth-wicket series partnership records, both set in 1982: 70 with Paul Allott v

India at Lord's and 79 with Bob Taylor v Pakistan at Edgbaston.

He was usually left not out when his partners attempted an improbable swipe knowing their time was limited. His best Test innings was when he forgot to take a bat with him.

Q My late father was given a bat by Tony Greig, after doing some plumbing for him, signed by that year's (1972) England players. There are two signatures that we cannot decipher. The ones we got are Boycott, Illingworth, Edrich, Snow, D'Oliveira, Willis, Knott, Underwood, Hampshire, Old, Arnold and Greig himself. The others appear as Barry Wood and something like Reg Murphy! **Paul**

BEARDERS' ANSWER: Sadly, my research will only compound the mystery. Barry Wood made his debut in the fifth Test. Others who represented England in that Ashes rubber were Brian Luckhurst, Norman Gifford, M.J.K. Smith, John Price, Peter Parfitt, Peter Lever and Keith Fletcher.

None of their signatures looks like 'Reg Murphy', although Parfitt's is hard to decipher. However, neither Chris Old nor Bob Willis played in that series so you now have the added problem of two signatures that should not be there!

Q My mother was to take me (aged three) to see Bradman's last innings at Worcester in 1948 but instead went into labour delivering my brother. He was born on 28 April 1948.

I have been led to believe that I missed a Bradman century and have yet to forgive my baby brother, Bob. What did Bradman score and was it on 28 April 1948? **Terry Jones, England**

BEARDERS' ANSWER: This is one of the more unusual questions that I've received during the first half-century of 'Ask Bearders', and I suspect it has almost elevated me to Agony Aunt status! I would have thought your parents were more culpable than brother Bob in the timing of his arrival.

'The Don' did indeed score a hundred (107) but it was on the second day, 29 April 1948. He gave his wicket away to conserve energy for the long tour ahead after a recent illness. His previous three visits to Worcester had produced scores of 236 (1930), 206 (1934), and 258 (1938).

Q I was briefly in the *TMS* [*Test Match Special* commentary] box for the Headingley Test as my dad knows CMJ [Christopher Martin-Jenkins] and I was going to ask you then, but you were too busy! To settle a debate, how tall is Alec Stewart? (He was sitting, so I couldn't gauge!) **Ben Winbolt-Lewis, England**

BEARDERS' ANSWER: I am beginning to suspect that CMJ only befriends folk with extended and hyphenated names. Unless he has shrunk since he retired from First-Class cricket, Alec Stewart is 5 feet 11 inches high.

 Can you list the record partnerships for each wicket by England? **Andrew Johnston, Sheffield, UK**

BEARDERS' ANSWER: Yes.

 Flintoff has three 'F's, Strauss has three 'S's, and Pietersen has three 'E's. Can you name the only English Test player with four of the same letter in his surname? **Andrew Race, Isle of Man**

BEARDERS' ANSWER: Are you a bored member of the Isle of Man Society of Chartered Accountants whom I will be addressing at a dinner next month?

Alan MULLALLY is alone among England's 634 Test cricketers to have four similar letters in his surname.

The Nawab of Pataudi, who played three Tests for England in the 1930s before captaining India against England in 1946, has four 'A's in his complete title but the family name (or surname) is Pataudi. 'Nawab' was the title given to Indian noblemen.

His full name was Iftikhar Ali Khan Pataudi. When the Indian government abolished the privy purse and all royal titles in 1971, his son, who captained Oxford University and India, became Mansur Ali Khan Pataudi.

Q The PCB has persuaded the ICC to change the result of the 2006 Oval Test from 'forfeiture' to draw. Your comments as a highly respected scorer and statistician on this will highly be appreciated. I know this was the only 'forfeited' Test in the history, but are there any other instances when the other results of Tests have been changed after so many days or months? **Bipin Dani (India)**

BEARDERS' ANSWER: There is no precedent for the result of a Test match being changed after the day of its completion, and this latest in a lengthening list of contentious and politically motivated decisions by the ICC has set an extremely dangerous precedent.

'Match forfeited' was the correct result under Law 21 when Pakistan refused to take the field with the England batsmen ready to play. The tourists' action cannot be excused by any evidence regarding the ball-tampering offence.

That was not the reason for the umpire's award of a forfeiture to England. Pakistan should have taken the field, completed the match, and then appealed against the ball-tampering decision through administrative channels. Law 21 (10) states that 'Once the umpires have agreed with the scorers the correctness of the scores at the conclusion of the match the result cannot thereafter be changed.' In my records, and in those of many other statisticians, this result will remain as a forfeited victory to England.

Q When Gooch got his 333 runs, I seem to remember Robin Smith using Gooch's bat for a short time after breaking his own. How many balls did he do this for? **Andyd2604**

BEARDERS' ANSWER: This occurred at 2.48pm on the second day of the 1990 Lord's Test against India. Smith borrowed Gooch's bat for precisely one ball – the fifth of Kapil Dev's 33rd over – and he didn't score off it.

Q Have you ever heard of a fielding position called a 'stray dog'?
A friend of mine recalls that stray dog originates from an old tea towel we had in our house when I was a kid. It described all the fielding positions on the cricket pitch, e.g. silly mid-on. 'Stray dog' was wandering around somewhere between wide third man and deep square cover!' **Jo Morley (Secretary, Haslemere CC)**

BEARDERS' ANSWER: Jo, I think you have answered your

own question. There is no such position! The stray dog was exactly that – a confused hound that had wandered onto the field when the artist was sketching the artwork for the teacloth.

When I looked at your club's website, I was relieved to discover that not only did Jack Hobbs and Arthur Conan Doyle play for you but that you are indeed Hon Secretary, Fixture Secretary and Scorer. I had suspected [fellow *TMS* commentator David] 'Bumble' Lloyd as being the originator of this question.

 Who was the last man given out by Dickie Bird in Test matches? **D. Lloyd, England**

BEARDERS' ANSWER: There are probably scores of 'D. Lloyd's at large in England, but I shall be very surprised if the perpetrator of this gem isn't the 'Bumble' who, besides representing and coaching England, was himself a First-Class umpire.

The last of 'Dickie' Bird's then record tally of 66 Tests was at Lord's in June 1996 when India drew the second contest of a three-match rubber.

My scoresheets show that the final wicket to fall from Bird's (Nursery) end was that of 'Jack' Russell who was adjudged lbw to an inswinger from Sourav Ganguly, having been hit in the box the ball before.

Why do they call David Lloyd 'Bumble'? **Edna Holland, England**

BEARDERS' ANSWER: Because his profile, involving a prominent proboscis, is not unlike that of animation characters called 'Bumblies' featured in one of the late Michael Bentine's children's television programmes.

 A friend and I were discussing hat-tricks and the likelihood of the same batsman being dismissed twice within the same hat-trick. Has this ever occurred at First-Class level? **Andrew Bak (Bradford)**

BEARDERS' ANSWER: I don't know of such an instance but, as hat-tricks can extend over both innings of a match (but not over successive matches), it is certainly possible.

When Australia's diminutive leg-spinner, Jimmy Matthews, took his two hat-tricks in separate innings at Old Trafford in the Triangular Tournament on the afternoon of 28 May 1912, his victims twice included wicket-keeper Tommy Ward. Apart from being the only batsman to feature in two hat-tricks on the same day, Ward is also the only Test cricketer to have been electrocuted while working in a gold mine.

Q While compiling statistics for Cleethorpes Cricket Club, our statistician found the instance of a Mr Lord, who collapsed and died of a heart attack whilst batting. The book recorded his departure 'retired dead', and his career average had been calculated with this counted as being out. Is this correct, or should a batsman retiring injured, or indeed dead, be counted as not out for such purposes? **Michael Shelton**

BEARDERS' ANSWER: Unless a batsman retires bored, his departure should be should recorded as 'retired not out'. This includes death and injury. It also includes compassionate retirements to visit seriously ill relatives or to accompany their pregnant wives to hospital ('retired to become a father').

Only voluntary retirements, when the batsman has no intention of resuming his innings, count as a wicket. All the others should be treated as 'not out' in calculating averages.

Q Regarding the number of ways that a batsman can be out, you didn't mention Absent. I recall poor Abdul Aziz being 'retired hurt' in the first innings of a match, and 'Absent Dead 0' in the second. If a batsman was Absent, I would record it as such in the scorebook, or would that now be classed as Timed Out? **Bill Benton (Nutley Hall CC, Surrey)**

BEARDERS' ANSWER: Timed out (Law 31) applies to an incoming batsman, who must be in a position to take guard, or ready for his partner to receive the next ball, within three minutes of the fall of the previous wicket. It does not apply to a batsman who, for whatever reason, is absent from the ground, or unable to bat through injury. If a batsman is absent he cannot be out because he was never going to begin his innings. A posthumous 'absent' is just a footnote. Incidentally, 'retired hurt' counts as a 'not out' innings in batting records.

Q At the start of one of our matches this season, our tall opening bowler ran in and bowled a fairly standard delivery. Immediately, the umpire ruled a no-ball, as our bowler had not stated his action to the umpire. This struck all of us as being incredibly petty, as we felt it was the role of the umpire to enquire as to the bowler's action. Having looked at Law 24 for a no-ball, it seems an umpire can give a no-ball if the bowler changes arm or side without informing the umpire, but states nothing about his first delivery.

Is it the role of the umpire or bowler to raise the issue, and therefore were we right to feel hard done by? **Paul (Surrey)**

BEARDERS' ANSWER: A fascinating question, Paul. As a bowler I cannot recall not being asked what I was going to bowl. My answers have varied from right-arm over to right-arm low stealth via right-arm filth. I did take a wicket bowling slow-left arm in the Australian outback but I did warn the umpire, who was on his tenth tinnie at the time. In fact, the notes to Law 16 on page 119 of Tom Smith's *New Cricket Umpiring and Scoring* include under 'Duties of Umpires Leading to Play Being Called': 'The bowler's end umpire should collect any items of clothing from the bowler and at the same time enquire as to his intended action.'

This is evidence that it is the umpire's duty to ascertain the bowler's action at the start of play and inform the batsman. Certainly a no-ball should not have been called.

Q My father-in-law, John Jameson, I know to be the first person to be run out in each innings of the same Test match. Recently he informed me that he was actually run out in three successive Test innings as he was also run out in his previous Test innings. Has anyone else managed this feat of being run out in three successive Test innings? **Paul Tregellas (Solihull)**

BEARDERS' ANSWER: By an extraordinary coincidence your father-in-law and I were seated either side of their president, Tom Graveney, last weekend at the 21st Anniversary Lunch of the Cricket Memorabilia Society.

In fact, John was the eleventh batsman to be run out

in both innings of a Test match but he remains the only one to suffer this fate for England. He is indeed the only one to have collected three run outs in successive Test innings – a unique hat-trick.

Australians seem especially adept at this form of dismissal as they are the victims of 418 (20.4%) of the 2,049 run outs in Tests. Allan Border (12) holds the record for being run out most often in a Test career. Mark Taylor and Ian Healy are alone in being run out in both innings of a Test on two occasions, while Jack Ryder was run out in both innings of his first match.

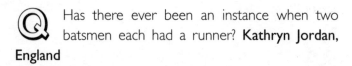

Has there ever been an instance when two batsmen each had a runner? **Kathryn Jordan, England**

BEARDERS' ANSWER: It is bound to have happened somewhere but I have never seen an instance. India came close to achieving it in their opening Test against England at Leeds in 1967. In the first innings both Rusi Surti (No. 9) and Bishan Bedi (No. 10) batted with runners but Robin Hobbs claimed his first Test wicket by dismissing Surti before Bedi could join him. India's captain, the Nawab of Pataudi ('Tiger'), predicted that had they batted together it was inevitable that all four batsmen would have ended up in the same crease – and he wanted a photograph.

Q Did P.G. Wodehouse name Bertie Wooster's valet, Jeeves, after a county cricketer? **Harry Webb (New York)**

BEARDERS' ANSWER: Yes, Wodehouse named him after Percy Jeeves, whom he saw playing for Warwickshire in 1913, two years before he introduced him to the public in 'Extricating Young Gussie'. Born in Dewsbury, Jeeves played 50 First-Class matches for Warwickshire (1912–1914), scoring 1,204 runs (average 16.05), the highest of his four fifties being 86 not out, and taking 199 wickets (average 20.03), including one 10-wicket haul and 12 five-wicket ones with his right-arm medium-fast bowling. He was killed in France in 1916 at the age of 28.

Q I won't ask you to name your all-time World Best XI, but would you pick Adam Gilchrist as keeper, as I suspect most would? Or would you select the best specialist keeper (mine would be Alan Knott)? **Chris Wheatley**

BEARDERS' ANSWER: As a former bowler I would certainly select the best gloveman. Only if their wicket-keeping skills were equal would I choose the better batsman. England's last two Test match keepers have cost England well in excess of 1,000 runs through missed chances. Such frequent errors demoralise bowlers who, in any event, are struggling to dismiss sides twice to win matches. Recent selections have confirmed a lack of confidence in England's specialist batsmen.

I certainly wouldn't pick Gilchrist, who is well down my list of Australia's best post-war keepers. Because there was little to choose between Godfrey Evans, Alan Knott and Bob Taylor as the best glovemen I have seen, I would agree with you and choose Knotty because he averaged 32.7 compared with Evans's 20.5 and Taylor's 16.2.

Q I know I must be being exceptionally dim but how can a bowler bowl an eight-ball maiden? **Paul Hartley**

BEARDERS' ANSWER: You have offered too little evidence to confirm your IQ, but you obviously have not heard of eight-ball overs which, in Test matches alone, were used in England (1939), Australia (1924–1925 and 1936–1937 to 1978–1979), South Africa (1938–1939 to 1957–1958), New Zealand (1968–1969 to 1978–1979), and Pakistan (1974–1975 to 1977–1978).

Q Why is Ashley Giles known as the 'King of Spain'? My friend has a theory about incorrectly spelt mugs but I am not so sure (if this is the case it would be the best story EVER!). **Dave Lane**

BEARDERS' ANSWER: Sadly, that is the answer. One of a batch of mugs inscribed 'King of Spin' below Ashley's portrait (mug shot?), ordered by the Warwickshire CCC shop, arrived with 'King of Spain' painted on it. Either inscription could have had the shop served with a false representation writ.

Q I've been trying to explain the idiosyncrasies of cricket to my girlfriend who seems to think they are proof that anyone who plays cricket is completely potty. I pointed out that although a Test match can last five days, it could be very short indeed. Ignoring declarations, forfeitures, retirements and absences, the shortest two innings game would be 31 balls: ten balls for each first innings, ten balls for the first side's second innings and a final ball for their opposition to score the winning run. What is the shortest ever Test match ever played? **Gareth (Kent)**

BEARDERS' ANSWER: A 31-ball four-innings match would be a scorer's nightmare and involve writing with both hands. In terms of both time (5 hours 53 minutes) and balls (656), the shortest Test match took place on a vicious Melbourne 'sticky' in February 1932. South Africa, who won the toss and batted, scored 36 and 45 in 89 and 105 minutes respectively. Australia, minus Bradman, who severely twisted his ankle when his studs caught in the coir matting of the dressing room as he was going out to field at the start, scored 153 in 159 minutes and won by an innings and 72 runs. South Africa's aggregate of 81 by a side losing all 20 wickets and the match aggregate of 234 remain records for Test cricket.

Q You may remember my father and your predecessor Arthur Wrigley. I still have his full library of books, including his Wisdens, which comprise reproductions of the first 15 years (given to me by Robert Hudson after my father died) and originals in a variety of conditions. You won't be surprised that some took a battering since they were very much tools of the job, and he was working before the electronic age.

I have stored this library in boxes for some 35 years and just having moved house feel that it would be a good time to sell them.

This is a long preamble to ask if you have any advice on how to sell them? **Steve Wrigley, England**

BEARDERS' ANSWER: What a wonderful surprise to hear from you, Steve. We met briefly at Didsbury in 1968 when I was playing in a benefit match for Ken Higgs at your father's old club. Arthur Wrigley, as *TMS* devotees will know, was the first to score a Test for the BBC Radio commentary team, a role he held virtually uninterrupted from 1934 until the end of the 1965 season when, in the words of Brian Johnston, 'the Great

Scorer summoned him.' I applied for the job and began the next summer on a three-match trial and was found not guilty!

All of your father's records and books would be valuable. You need to compile a catalogue of them, noting the condition of the books. You can then approach either an auction house – Christies have conducted several auctions of cricketana in recent years – or canvass the second-hand book dealers, many of whom advertise in the cricket monthlies and annuals. I would certainly be interested in seeing the list if you care to send it to me via TMS, Room 5016, BBC TV Centre, LONDON W12 7RJ.

(Q) When scoring, do you mark recent innovations such as powerplays? I wondered, as during England's recent internationals, Swann's figures outside the powerplay overs were very respectable. In future, comparing the career of someone whose figures were achieved before such changes with someone afterwards might be unfair. **Adrian Worley**

BEARDERS' ANSWER: I did record them when I scored limited-overs matches, simply by ruling off those sections of the linear scoresheet. Someone may feel the urge to compile the stats you suggest but it won't be me!

Is there any bowler who took wickets bowling left handed and right handed? **Murthy Dasika, United States**

BEARDERS' ANSWER: In the same match? Well, I did when I captained an 'England XI' in a Bush Ashes game at Tilpa (official population eight) in remotest New South Wales on 8 January 1983. We played on a matting-on-concrete pitch in an arena of red sand.

As the temperature was 40C, we had drinks breaks every four overs. I opened the bowling right arm medium-fast off a 20-yard run, taking a wicket – and a long break – before returning and taking another wicket bowling slow left-arm!

Fred Trueman could bowl very accurate left-arm spin and Brian Close was ambidextrous, but I don't think either employed it at First-Class level. Hanif Mohammed bowled three balls of an over right-handed and the remainder with his left, possibly against Somerset at Taunton in 1967.

 Adam Gilchrist used to wear a squash ball in his batting gloves. Is that legal? **slowerball**

BEARDERS' ANSWER: There is nothing in the Laws of Cricket to prevent you putting anything inside your batting glove and you can wear as many pairs of gloves as you like.

The same applies to wicket-keeping gloves – many of the old-timers used to put steaks inside the palms of the gloves before inners were invented. Probably an extra bionic hand, giving a three-handed grip on the bat, would be considered against the spirit of cricket though.

Q Bill, can you offer some comment on bat technology? Through the 1970s and 1980s there was a plethora of bat types, such as the scoop, double scoop, flat back, super short steel spring, perimeter weighted and of course the aluminium-skinned bat.

I haven't been able to identify any current international batsman using anything other than the stock standard design (certainly bat weights vary). Were these all flash-in-the-pan gimmicks, and is the standard design simply superior? **Cameron, Australia**

BEARDERS' ANSWER: A very interesting question, Cameron, but not really related to my statistical domain. If a bat manufacturer files some comments we will reveal them.

Apart from Dennis Lillee's aluminium bat being used for four balls against England at Perth on 14 December 1979, I don't recall many of these oddities being used at Test level. Bob Willis used a bat with several holes drilled through its blade but it did not noticeably improve his performance with the willow. I wouldn't have noticed it if he hadn't walked out to bat without it in one Test match!

Q At the start of a match we, as the bowling side, waited to see which batsman was facing and then chose our bowler. The batsmen then changed over so that the other batsman was to face the first ball. So we changed our bowler. The impasse was only resolved by our giving in and naming our opening bowler before letting the opposition choose which of their opening batsmen faced first. Who really should choose first? **Chrisnicolbeyond**

BEARDERS' ANSWER: There is nothing in the Laws to deal with such nonsense apart from it contravening the Spirit of Cricket. The fielding captain, usually after discussing preference of ends with his opening bowlers, decides from which end play will begin and advises the umpires. The batsmen then go to their chosen ends. Normally they would choose who wanted to face the first ball – not which bowler they didn't want to face.

Q a) I am very interested in sport statistics and would like to find a career in this field. What is the best way to go about it, Bill? Your comments would be very useful.

b) Of the Test batsmen who have played more than 50 Tests, who has the lowest average? **Sam, England**

BEARDERS' ANSWER: a) Build up a sports library of reference books, join some sports statistics associations (e.g. The Association of Cricket Statisticians and Historians), involve yourself with your local sports clubs, contribute features to your local newspaper and radio station – and read the obituaries carefully!

b) Bhagwat Chandrasekhar, the leg-break and googly bowler who took 242 wickets for India between 1963–1964 and 1979, holds that record. In 80 innings during 58 Tests he scored 167 runs at an average of 4.07.

Q I am wondering if you are still playing for Urchfont CC? About 15 years ago, I faced you during a match at Bath Cricket Club. I later umpired in the match and when you came on to bowl again, I said 'new bowler' to the batsman, to which you replied, 'Thank you for the NEW!' **Alex Durrans, France**

BEARDERS' ANSWER: Sorry the experience caused you to flee across the Channel. I seldom play now, but last Sunday I did extend my career by appearing in a match at Surrey's Banstead CC where I enjoyed my first decade of club cricket as a bowler rather than as a notcher.

If you were to compile a list of players gaining just one cap for England, who would be in the team? **Robert Lawrie, UK**

BEARDERS' ANSWER: No fewer than 86 players have made a solitary Test match appearance for England.

From that massive list, my opening batsmen would be Dennis Brookes (Northamptonshire) and George Emmett (Gloucestershire).

The wicket-keeper would be 'Hopper' Levett of Kent, and the opening bowlers two men of genuine pace in 'Hopper' Read (Essex) and Jack Martin (Kent). Jim Parks senior would be the all-rounder.

Spin would be in the capable hands of Walter Mead (Essex – off-breaks) and Charlie Parker (Gloucestershire – orthodox left-arm). Sir Aubrey 'Round-the-Corner' Smith (Sussex), the Hollywood actor who uniquely led England in his only Test, would be my captain.

The side would be completed by two Australian Test cricketers who appeared once for England – the left-handed John 'J.J.' Ferris and the legendary Billy Murdoch. The latter, the outstanding Aussie batsman of his era, was the first to score 200 in a Test, the first captain to score a Test hundred and the first substitute to hold a catch – a feat he achieved for the opposition!

Can you tell me why 111 is referred to as Nelson? **John Baldwin, England**

BEARDERS' ANSWER: Yes. The polite answer is that it refers to his three major sea victories: Aboukir Bay, Copenhagen and Trafalgar. The more common reference involves one eye, one arm and one etcetera!

Q Were the Aussies the first to introduce the practice of sledging their opponents? **George, Australia**

BEARDERS' ANSWER: According to most players I have spoken to in the last 30 years, sledging began in the Packer era when players were encouraged to ham it up for the TV audience.

Prior to that there had always been banter, witticisms and subtle asides from one fielder to another intended for the batsmen to overhear and to upset his concentration. Not direct personal abuse though. Far be it for me to award an accolade for the instigator!

Q Seeing that Jason Krejza was dropped after his Test debut, albeit tactically, I was wondering, if he never plays again for Australia, would he have the best 'single Test' figures ever? **Stuart, West Bromwich**

BEARDERS' ANSWER: Yes, he would, but it would be a major surprise if he were not to appear shortly against

South Africa. No other bowler has taken 12 wickets in a single-Test career.

Charles Stowell ('Father') Marriott, who took 11 for 96 (5-37 and 6-59) for England against West Indies at The Oval in August 1933, is the only other one-Test wonder to have taken more than seven wickets. Marriott, a tall right-arm leg-break and googly bowler, began his goose-stepping run at mid-off. He turned the ball sharply from a high action, his delivery arm starting its swing from behind his back like Jeff Thomson.

Although his solitary appearance, when nearing his 38th birthday, scuppered West Indies by an innings in two days and ten minutes, Marriott was an appalling fielder and batsman (574 runs as opposed to 711 wickets in 159 First-Class matches for Lancashire, Cambridge University and Kent). He was unlikely to have inflicted too much damage on the enemy during his Second World War duties as a Home Guard anti-aircraft gunner.

Q Growing up in the West Indies, I sometimes heard the term 'square maiden' as applied to a bowler's performance. I never understood what the term meant and it seems to have disappeared from the lexicon of modern cricket. Any illumination as to what it meant? **Nari Rampersad, Canada**

BEARDERS' ANSWER: Nari, I have never heard the term

'square maiden' and it does not rate a mention in Michael Rundell's exhaustive and comprehensive *Dictionary of Cricket*. It might have derived from the days of four-ball overs which would have been recorded within squares in the scorebook. A maiden could have been emphasised by joining the dots into a square, similar to the dots of six-ball maidens being joined as an M (or W for a wicket-maiden). On the other hand, it could have referred to the shape of the bowler!

On the Ump

Q When there is a run out and both batsmen are stranded at one end of the wicket (and assuming they are level with each other relative to the wicket), are they allowed to decide between themselves who will sacrifice himself? **Lilia Aird**

BEARDERS' ANSWER: No, the umpires must decide according to Law 38 (Run Out), (3 – Which Batsman is Out?). It would depend on which wicket was broken and the decision would vary according to the number of runs taken. For example, if just one run was attempted by the striker, without the non-striker leaving his crease, and the wicket was broken at the non-striker's (bowler's) end with both batsmen in the crease, then the striker would be out.

There was a fluke instance in a limited-overs international between England and West Indies at Scarborough when a return from the boundary broke both wickets (through a ricochet from one set of stumps to the other) while both batsmen were stranded in mid-wicket.

After much discussion the confused umpires gave neither batsman out!

Q If an umpire loses count and only five balls are bowled, does this still count as an over for statistical purposes? **David Coleman, England**

BEARDERS' ANSWER: Yes, whatever number of legitimate balls are bowled before 'over' is called, that tally will constitute the over. I have frequently scored five- and seven-ball overs in Test cricket. In the first Test between New Zealand and England at Auckland's Eden Park in February 1963, umpire R.W.R. ('Dick') Shortt allowed off-spinner John Sparling to bowl an 11-ball over (excluding no-balls and wides). The actual number of balls bowled in a rogue over should be recorded in the innings tallies of the batsman and the team.

Q Is there a law that says if a batsman is given out on ball seven of an erroneous seven-ball over that if he points this out, he will be allowed to stay in? **maw501**

BEARDERS' ANSWER: No.

Q When one says 'a batsman was out without troubling the scorers', how much trouble does the batsman really cause? **Aaron van Geordieland**

BEARDERS' ANSWER: Frequently I have publicly threatened to throttle any commentator who uses that hackneyed and erroneous expression. The fall of a wicket produces pressure points in any scoring system. If wickets fall in swift succession that pressure is dramatically increased.

The linear method I have designed for *TMS* commentaries involves three A4 sheets: the Ball-by-Ball Record of Play, the Innings Scorecard and the Cumulative Bowling Analyses. Only the first two are immediately affected by the fall of a wicket. First I stop the watch, recording the length of his innings and zero it for the new batsman.

Record of Play: I enter 'W' in the dismissed batsman's column to show which ball took his wicket and the time of his dismissal on the next line of the 'time' column. I complete all totals in the 'End-of-Over' section and the outgoing batsman's balls and boundaries columns. Then I rule off that batsman's section and his column in the 'Totals' section. The new batsman's name is then entered on the next line of the batting column.

Innings Scorecard: I enter details of that batsman's dismissal (time out, minutes batted, how out, runs, fall-of-wicket, fours, sixes and balls faced) and his partnership details (runs, minutes and balls). Finally I add the new batsman's name and enter the time he went in.

In Test matches there would normally be a two-minute hiatus before play is resumed but it is far shorter in limited-overs games and virtually non-existent in the 20-over format.

(Q) Among the rarer forms of dismissal, I remember seeing Desmond Haynes, Graham Gooch and Steve Waugh given handled ball, but has any batsman ever been timed out or dismissed for obstruction in Tests? **Craig, England**

BEARDERS' ANSWER: No one has been timed out in a Test match, but Len Hutton was given out for obstructing the field at the Oval in 1951 when a ball from off-spinner Athol Rowan ballooned up from the bat's top edge and Hutton, in fending it off his stumps, prevented South Africa's wicket-keeper, Russell Endean, from making a catch.

In addition to the three batsmen you mention, Russell Endean, Andrew Hilditch, Mohsin Khan and Michael Vaughan have been dismissed for handling the ball in a Test.

(Q) The score is 8 for no wicket after the first over. This over consisted of four dot balls and then two run-scoring shots. At the end of the over both batsmen were on 4 not out. How? **Jon Steane, England**

BEARDERS' ANSWER: The first batsman hits a ball into the deep; they run five including overthrows but that tally includes one short run. Having crossed, the second batsman then hits a boundary.

Q In a recent game, incidentally on the Balmoral estate, I bowled a delivery, which pitched on a normal length but then proceeded to roll along the ground without bouncing.

Of course, under modern rules this has to be taken as a no-ball, even though it bounced only a couple of feet in front of the batsman. To add to my woe, the ball beat the keeper and landed in a spare helmet lying behind him. Given that I bowled a no-ball, do the five penalty runs go against the bowlers' analysis or not? **Gordon Anderson, Scotland**

BEARDERS' ANSWER: The five penalty runs are not debited against the bowler's analysis. Under the 2000 Code of Laws such penalties are recorded as a fifth category of extras or sundries, joining byes, leg-byes, wides and no-balls. There have already been numerous instances of five penalty runs appearing in the breakdown of extras at all levels of the game.

Q Is there any cricketing significance in umpire David Shepherd's ritual relating to scores or intervals of 111 runs? **Damian Brewitt, Dorset, UK**

BEARDERS' ANSWER: None – research has proved that no more wickets fall at team or individual totals of 111 and its multiples than at any other number. The total at which most batsmen are out is 0! It is a totally irrational superstition, and cricketers are prey to a great many such terrors. The Australians observe 87 (13 off 100) as their devil's number.

David Shepherd's antics evolved from players trying to keep their feet off the ground when 111 appears on the scoreboard. Much easier when one is seated unless levitation has been mastered.

Q I imagine you are not fond of all the new innovations in modern limited-overs cricket. One of those I only heard of recently, is the 'free hit'. When did it first appear? How do you show it in your scoring system? **Aaron (Newcastle upon Tyne, ex-Johannesburg)**

BEARDERS' ANSWER: Yes, I have always favoured old innovations! The 'free hit' awarded in addition to a runs penalty for over-stepping no-balls has been with us for ten English seasons. It was introduced by the ECB in 1999 and was restricted to games in the CGU

National Cricket League when the 'Sunday League' was reinvented as a 45-over two-division competition. I note it on my linear scoring system with a dagger against the runs scored off the free-hit ball and a corresponding 'FH' in notes column alongside.

Q In the 2001 Ashes series, Steve Bucknor and John Holder officiated in the Lord's Test. Could you confirm if that was the first time two West Indian-born umpires stood simultaneously in a Test in England? **Earl W. Robinson, St. Vincent & the Grenadines, W.I.**

BEARDERS' ANSWER: Good to hear from you Earl (an enthusiastic correspondent and supplier of exotic stamps for many years).

Holder's previous ten Tests (six in England and four in Pakistan with John Hampshire) had all been in partnership with English-born umpires. Bucknor and Holder are certainly the first pair of black umpires to officiate in a Test in England. I don't know the birthplaces of all the early umpires who officiated in Tests in England so it is possible that one might have been born in the West Indies – after all, two England captains, Lord Harris and Sir Pelham Warner, were born in Trinidad.

Q I am an Englishman currently playing cricket in Australia, and I was shocked last week when a local came up and told me I was filling in my scorebook incorrectly. I am told that Australians mark a wicket with an X, and wides with a W – whereas I was always taught the other way round in England. What is the 'accepted' international convention – and why has/when did this difference arise? **Ausbantam**

BEARDERS' ANSWER: Stick to W for wicket and a plus sign for wides. Never heard such nonsense! Australians do tend to be confused through having to spend their lives the wrong way up.

Q I recently watched highlights of the England v South Africa world cup game in 1992 where, under the rain rule, South Africa's winning target was modified from 22 off 13 balls to 21 off one ball. What would the target have been under the Duckworth/Lewis rule? **philosophicalRourkey**

BEARDERS' ANSWER: In that World Cup day/night semi-final at Sydney on 22 March, England scored 252-6 in an innings reduced from 50 to 45 overs because of South Africa's tardy bowling rate. The D/L Method would have set Kepler Wessels' team a revised target of 273 off 45 overs but the current rules let them off with 20 runs fewer. Having reached 231-6 after 42.5 overs, South Africa's reply was interrupted by 12 minutes of heavy rain. Under the 'rain rule' governing this tournament, they initially needed 22 off seven balls but this was adjusted to 21 off one.

Using the current version of the D/L Method and ignoring the five overs lost to slow bowling, South Africa were 22 short of their initial target of 253 when the break came and were just three runs behind par. If two overs had been deducted under the D/L Method, Brian McMillan would have needed to score five runs off that final ball.

Q What is the difference between a run out and a stumping? In a recent match the batsman missed the ball and the keeper was standing back. The batsman went out of his crease and the keeper threw the ball and hit the stumps. Was this a run out or a stumping? The bowler wants to know if it is his wicket (stumping) or just a run out. **Oldkev**

BEARDERS' ANSWER: Law 39 stipulates that only the wicket-keeper can stump a batsman. If the dismissal occurs after the ball has made contact with another member of the fielding side, the dismissal is classed as run out. As the keeper can kick or throw the ball onto the stumps, or rebound it off his body or pads, the dismissal you describe was a stumping and should be credited to the bowler.

Q I was interested to hear (on **TMS** at Lord's) you immediately informed the commentator on demand that Jamie How was dropped on 42 (I believe). Was this an act of memory, a separate note or is it officially included within the scoring notes? **Peter (Norfolk)**

BEARDERS' ANSWER: My vertical linear scoring system, has a notes column for each over. In this I can record many happenings, including dropped catches. A symbol in Jamie How's column against the sixth ball of Stuart Broad's fifth over refers to a note reading 'Dropped 1st slip (Strauss) – head-high'. From the other columns I can reveal that the chance occurred at 12.17pm on the fifth day and that How had then scored 46 of New Zealand's 75 for 2 after 30 overs.

Q Playing in the Dordogne last summer, the opposition bowler was several times no-balled for sending down bouncers well over our opener's head. The youngster eventually 'up periscoped' and holed out. He then held his ground claiming that 'no-ball' had been called (which it had been) but was still given out. The umpire claimed it wasn't a no-ball if he could hit it. Who was right? **James**

BEARDERS' ANSWER: Your umpire was correct in calling 'no-ball' (rather than 'wide') under Law 42.6 (a) (ii) which covers Dangerous and Unfair Bowling – Bowling of fast short-pitched balls. However, he has confused the laws concerning wides and no-balls. Although an umpire's call of 'wide' must be rescinded if the batsman hits the ball, this does not apply to no-balls.

Q How do you enter a no-ball correctly in a scorebook? I was under the impression that it's a circle, and when the ball is bowled legally the result is then entered inside. Hope you can help me out. **Jon Martin, Kent, England**

BEARDERS' ANSWER: Enter a circle to record the penalty run for a no-ball. If the batsman hits the no-ball for additional runs these are recorded within the circle. If the batsmen run 'byes' or 'leg-byes' off a no-ball, each of those runs is recorded as a dot within the circle and they count as additional no-balls (not as byes or leg-byes).

Q What happens if the fielding team needs one wicket to win, and the batting team needs one run to draw or win, and the batsman is stumped off a wide? **Andy Lake**

BEARDERS' ANSWER: Law 25, note 3 (a) decrees that,

although an umpire cannot determine if a ball is a wide until it passes the striker's wicket, once he has called it, it is considered to have been a wide from the moment of delivery. In your scenarios, the batting side has gained a penalty run for the wide and, at that point, they have drawn or won the match. The 'stumping' occurred after the match was over and is not relevant to the action.

Q Has a Test batsman ever been given out 'timed out'? I have only just learnt about this 2-minute rule. **Andy Parsons, UK**

BEARDERS' ANSWER: Not in Test matches, but there has been one instance in First-Class cricket and it occurred on 20 December 1997, the final day of a Ranji Trophy East Zone match between Orissa and Tripura at the Barabati Stadium in Cuttack, India. A drinks break was taken when Tripura's ninth wicket fell at 10.28am and their number 11, one Hemulal Yadav, sat near the boundary but made no effort to go to the crease until 10.33am, after the drinks had been taken off the ground. Orissa appealed, and the umpires (Dr K.N. Raghvan and S. Dendapani, both from Kerala) upheld the appeal.

Q I was playing in a recent amateur league match in Edinburgh when an unusual situation arose. Very strong winds meant that the bails kept being blown off. Having no heavy bails, a decision was made to play on without bails at all. The opposition ninth batsman was subsequently given out when the ball looped up off his pad and trickled onto the stumps at a speed almost certainly too gentle to have dislodged the bails. Was this decision correct? Also what would happen in First-Class or Test cricket were the use of bails impossible? Would play stop? **John Logan (Edinburgh)**

BEARDERS' ANSWER: Law 8 (note 5), which applies to all levels of cricket, allows the umpires to dispense with bails if heavier (lignum vitae) ones are unavailable. They must be dispensed with at BOTH ends and replaced as soon as conditions permit. This has occurred in First-Class and Test cricket but not often because umpires usually carry a set of heavy bails.

In your match, the decision was correct because in those circumstances (Law 28, note 4) the wicket is deemed to have been 'put down' if the umpire concerned is satisfied that the wicket has been struck by the ball. Its velocity is irrelevant.

Q Say a team needs one run to win, and the batsman hits the ball towards the boundary but runs the required single before the ball reaches the rope; only one run is awarded as the match is said to have been completed once that run has been completed, correct? What, then, would happen should one run be required to win, the ball is hit very high in the air, the batsmen complete a run, but the ball is caught by a fielder? When does the match end? **Tom Hicks, Herefordshire**

BEARDERS' ANSWER: One run is indeed the correct answer to your first example. In your second one, the dismissal ends the match (with a win for the fielding team) regardless of how many runs have been taken before the catch was completed. Law 32 (2): 'Runs completed by the batsmen before the completion of the catch will not be scored.'

Q In terms of stats, when is a batsman deemed to have actually batted? When a ball is bowled whilst he is in the middle or when he faces any ball? In the recent Wellington Test, did Chris Martin technically 'bat' in the final innings? He faced nothing at all, but he was there in the middle for at least 30 seconds while the match was in progress. **Chris, Birmingham**

BEARDERS' ANSWER: Law 10 (Commencement of a Batsman's Innings) decrees that, except at the start of play, a batsman's innings begins when he first steps onto the field of play, provided 'Time' has not been called. The innings of opening batsmen, and that of any new batsman at the resumption of play after a call of 'Time', shall commence at the call of 'Play'.

Ⓠ In Pakistan's first innings, Wasim Akram was hit on the helmet and the ball went for four leg-byes. Why was that allowed since Wasim was obviously taking evasive action and not playing a shot?

Is the law different depending on where it hits the body? Since if it hits the pads a shot must have been played for a run to count. **Nigel Marchant, England**

BEARDERS' ANSWER: Yes. Law 26.2(ii) awards leg-byes if 'the umpire is satisfied that the striker has tried to avoid being hit by the ball'. As Wasim obviously didn't deliberately head the ball, leg-byes were correctly awarded.

Ⓠ How many bowlers have bowled six byes? I believe there was an Essex bowler early in the twentieth century called Charles Kortwright who did this. Are there more? **Andrew Bain, UK**

BEARDERS' ANSWER: Good trick question, Andrew! The answer is none, unless they involved overthrows. Many considered Kortright (no W) the fastest bowler ever to appear in county cricket (1894–1907), and he may well have bowled a bouncer that cleared the rope. However, a ball which pitches and carries the boundary without bouncing or being intercepted by the batsman scores FOUR byes – or, more appropriately as it probably passed the batsman well clear of his reach, four WIDES.

Only HITS that clear the boundary can score six.

In 1967 I set a question for the BBC Radio quiz show *Sporting Chance* which caused a certain amount of havoc because it had to be taken out of the recording and an alternative substituted: How does an umpire signal six byes? My answer was with three arms. Don Mosey was very upset with me!

Q What would happen if a bowler could not carry on mid-over because of injury? Would another bowler take his place? **Patrick, England**

BEARDERS' ANSWER: Yes. Another bowler would complete the over. This has frequently happened at all levels of the game. In limited-overs cricket, the shared over counts as one of the side's overall entitlement (50 in internationals) but the bits count as full overs in the two bowlers' ration (10 overs in internationals).

I would like to know how scorers would record the following incident:

Batsman glances the ball off his legs and it hits the helmet behind the wicket keeper. Under the new law (2000 Code), will it be recorded as five penalty runs (Under Law 42) or will it be five runs to the batsman?

Also, what would the case be if it hits the helmet without hitting the striker's bat? **Arun Kumar, India**

BEARDERS' ANSWER: Whether or not the batsman has hit it, if the ball comes into contact with a fielder's helmet parked behind the wicket-keeper it becomes dead and a penalty of five runs is awarded to the batting side. No penalty is awarded if the ball has touched the batsman's clothing (other than his glove) when he was not playing a stroke or trying to avoid the ball.

Penalties are a form of extras – not credited to the batsman nor debited to the bowler. In my linear scoring system I would put a 'P' above the dot recording that ball with an explanation in the 'NOTES' column.

Is a batsman allowed to knock the ball away from his stumps if it is heading towards him having already been hit? If so, and were the second hit to be caught, is that out? **Glenn Matthews, England**

BEARDERS' ANSWER: Law 34 covers Hitting the Ball Twice. Note 3 says: 'Solely in order to guard his wicket and before the ball has been touched by any fielder, the striker may lawfully strike the ball more than once with his bat or with any part of his person other than a hand not holding the bat.' Provided that the ball had not touched the ground after the first hit he could be caught off the second.

(Q) I was playing in a match where the bowler, during his delivery stride, accidentally broke the wicket with his hand at the non-striker's end. The batsman was caught out off this delivery but the umpire signalled a no-ball because the stumps had been broken.

Was this the correct decision? And has ever such an incident been recorded in First-Class cricket? **HawaiianExpress**

BEARDERS' ANSWER: Bowlers often accidentally break the non-striker's wicket with their hand or even foot as they are delivering the ball. It certainly is not a no-ball and the batsman in your match should have been given out. In exceptional circumstances an umpire can call 'dead ball'.

(Q) In a one-day international, if a team needs one run to win with one wicket remaining, what happens if the next ball is a wide, but the batsman is stumped? **Paul H, England**

BEARDERS' ANSWER: As in any level of cricket, the ball is dead once the winning run(s) have been scored so the stumping doesn't count.

Q Last night I had a discussion with an Aussie friend who claimed that there were only seven ways to get out at cricket. But I'm sure I remember a question in Trivial Pursuit that claimed there were 11 or 12. Can you resolve this so we can at least beat an Aussie at something this summer! **Andrea Jacobs, France**

BEARDERS' ANSWER: There are ten: bowled, caught, stumped, lbw, run out, hit wicket, handled the ball, hit the ball twice, obstruction of the field and timed out.

Q What is the stumping rule related to a wicket keeper who has accidentally knocked the bails off with his pad while attempting to run out a batsman. How does he redeem the wicket if there is enough time? **Ian, South Africa**

BEARDERS' ANSWER: He has to break the wicket with the ball – he can deflect it with his pad or any part of his person or protective equipment other than his helmet.

If he breaks the wicket (i.e. removes both bails) without the ball, then he has to pull up a stump with the ball in his glove(s) – not easy.

Q Can both batsmen be run out off the same ball? If so, has it ever happened in a Test match? **Chris Wheatley, New Zealand**

BEARDERS' ANSWER: No. The ball becomes dead as soon as the first one is run out.

In a limited-overs international between England and West Indies on 26 August 1976 at Scarborough, Michael Holding's return from long-leg deflected off the nearer wicket and scuttled along the pitch to break the far one with Graham Barlow and Alan Knott (on his only appearance as England's captain) by then in mid-pitch. The dumbfounded umpires (W.E. Alley and A.E. Fagg) rejected the run out appeal!

Q What calculation do they use to find out how many runs are needed to avoid the follow-on? **Toby Kendall, England**

BEARDERS' ANSWER: It varies according to the length of the match. The minimum required leads for the follow-on to be enforced are: One-day match: 75 runs. 2 days:

100 runs. Three or four days: 150 runs. Five or more days: 200 runs.

 Is it possible to get two batsmen out in one ball (e.g. a catch, then a run out)? **James, Middlesex**

BEARDERS' ANSWER: No. Under Law 23 (iii) the ball becomes dead when a batsman is dismissed. The fielding side can dismiss only one batsman from any one delivery.

 I see that in the Twenty20 games there is a tendency for the boundaries to be brought in to encourage more fours and sixes. Are there any rules as to the minimum and maximum distances for boundaries in any form of the game? **John (Dudley)**

BEARDERS' ANSWER: The ECB's Regulations and Playing Conditions covering all domestic competitions stipulate that 'The Ground Authority shall aim to provide the largest playing area, subject to no boundary exceeding a distance of 90 yards from the centre of the pitch. No boundary shall be less than 50 yards.'

Q In a recent county match, a hit to long-on landed on the sponsor's triangular cover placed over the boundary rope. I thought that to be a six a ball had to clear the boundary rope, not hit it. In this case the third umpire ruled it a six. Was this correct? **Simon (Colchester)**

BEARDERS' ANSWER: Yes, the umpire was correct. Law 19 covers boundaries in great detail. The boundary is part of the line or rope that is closest to the umpires. As soon as the ball touches any part of it a boundary is scored. The allowance of four or six runs depends on whether the ball touches the ground before reaching the boundary (4) or lands on or beyond it (6).

Q What constitutes 'hitting the ball twice'? In a game I played in last season, a batsman played a short ball that then began rolling back towards his stumps; he proceeded to hit the ball away from the stumps, which we thought meant he had hit the ball twice and should have been dismissed. The umpire (one of their players), said that the batsman was not out. Was this the correct decision? **Bhav (London)**

BEARDERS' ANSWER: Yes, it was correct. Law 34 allows a batsman to hit the ball a second time in order to guard his wicket or return the ball to a fielder.

Ⓠ Consider the following situation. The side batting first in a one-day match gets bowled out relatively cheaply (eg for 150). The side batting second gets off to a flier and are 100/0 in the tenth over.

The bowler then notices some dark clouds looming and proceeds to deliberately bowl a series of wides in the hope that rain arrives before 10 overs are bowled and the D/L system can determine a result.

Is there anything in the laws of the game for an umpire to intervene, i.e. to deliberately not call a wide? **Tony**

BEARDERS' ANSWER: The Laws of Cricket do not specifically deal with such an instance. It depends how imminent the rain is, but the umpire could just allow the bowler to send down 50 wides and gift the match. Some wides might elude the wicket-keeper and concede five runs. Depending on the length of his run, the bowler would probably take about 20 minutes to achieve this surrender.

Alternatively, the umpire could interpret this ploy as being in breach of the Spirit of the Game, and, after warning the bowler and his captain, invoke Law 42 (Fair and Unfair Play).

Ⓠ Relating to a previous question about the number of ways that a batsman may be dismissed, is there a cricket equivalent to football's 'Red Card'? **AsleepAtThirdMan**

BEARDERS' ANSWER: In soccer, the referee's award of a red card ejects the recipient from the game and he may not be replaced. There is no equivalent in cricket. Umpires can report a player's bad conduct to his fellow umpire. They can then jointly advise his captain of the offence and instruct him to take action. In extreme cases the captain has then ordered the offending player off the field. Umpires can also report a grave offence to the Executive of the player's team and any governing body responsible for the match.

Stats Cricket

How many runs (approx.) have been scored over the history of First-Class and Test cricket? It must be in the millions. Likewise wickets – must be many thousands. I'm fascinated by the potential scale of the aggregates. **DoctorQuelch**

BEARDERS' ANSWER: The Test match aggregates, courtesy of Ric Finlay, are currently (20 September 2008) 1,833,354 runs and 57,672 wickets.

Alas, unlike Test cricket's 15 March 1877, there is no specific date upon which First-Class cricket can be said to have begun. The term 'First-Class' was not introduced until the 1840s, Although the Association of Cricket Statisticians and Historians has published a First-Class Match List starting with the 1801 season, it recognises that matches played prior to 1864 should be termed 'Important' or 'Great'. Philip Bailey has revealed that the First-Class aggregates from 1864 until after play on 20 September 2008 are 39,211,720 runs and 1,462,286 wickets from 49,709 matches. If you start with the 1801 season (50,725 matches), you have 39,637,638 runs and 1,497,951 wickets. The Test match tallies are included in those figures.

Q On which overseas ground have England won the most Test matches? My guess would be Sydney, or another Australian ground. **Cabbagehead**

BEARDERS' ANSWER: Your guessing ability is far superior to your choice of an alias! England's most successful overseas grounds are Sydney (21 wins) and Melbourne (19). England have played 53 Tests on each. Five of the six English grounds on which 30 or more home Tests have been played have not surprisingly produced most England victories: Lord's (43 wins, 115 Tests), the Oval (36, 91), Headingley (30, 68), Old Trafford (24, 72), Edgbaston (22, 43). The exception is Trent Bridge, where England have won only 17 of their 54 Tests.

Q A chap in our team is currently undergoing a miserable run of form. He has two consecutive golden ducks, and we were wondering who had the record for the most number of consecutive ducks in Test cricket? **Blaggers12**

BEARDERS' ANSWER: The most ducks in successive Test innings is five, an unfortunate record shared by three bowlers. R.G. ('Bob') Holland of Australia was the first with consecutive pairs against England (1985) and New Zealand (1985–1986). Then India's A.B. (Ajit) Agarkar, scorer of a Test hundred at Lord's, registered four successive noughts in two Tests against Australia (1999–2000). The most recent instance was inflicted upon Pakistan's Mohammad Asif in three separate series (2005–2006 and 2006).

Q About 15 years ago, I played for the same club as Surendra Bhave of Maharashtra and West Zone, a very fine player. Is there anyone in world cricket who has scored more First-Class runs at a higher average than 'Surrey' and never represented his country? **David McKay, England**

BEARDERS' ANSWER: Thank you for a fascinating question, David. Surendra Shriram Bhave played in 97 First-Class matches between 1986–1987 and 2000–2001 inclusive, scoring 7,971 runs at 58.18 with 28 hundreds, 27 fifties and a highest score of 292 for West Zone against South Zone at Rourkela in 1994–1995.

Four British batsmen exceeded Bhave's aggregate without playing international Test cricket, but none approached his average. They are Alan Jones of Glamorgan (36,049 runs at 32.89) who played for England against Rest of the World in 1970, and was awarded a cap for an appearance in a match subsequently ruled by the ICC as unofficial, John Langridge of Sussex (34,380 at 37.45), Les Berry of Leicestershire (30,225 at 30.25) and Ken Suttle of Sussex (also 30,225, at 31.09).

Very few batsmen have averaged over 58 in their First-Class career, and I haven't located one who did not play Test cricket. I wondered if B.B. Nimbalkar had done so. Although he is the only batsman to score a quadruple hundred (443 not out) and not play Test cricket, both his aggregate (4,841 in 80 matches) and average (47.93) are inferior to those of Bhave.

Q My question concerns Test batsmen who have reached centuries via the hitting of a maximum (six runs). While I assume this is done more frequently these days than in the past, I have no idea whether this list contains four or 40 names. How many batsmen have performed this feat? Has anybody ever done it more than once? **Eric Perez**

BEARDERS' ANSWER: The list of batsman completing a Test hundred with a six currently contains 84 instances. As some scorebooks have been lost or destroyed (there is a suspicious lack of entries between 1898 and 1922) this is unlikely to be a complete dossier. Ken Barrington and Sachin Tendulkar have achieved the feat four times. Aravinda de Silva and Brian Lara have done it on three occasions. Seven others have done it twice.

Q Apparently New Zealand's Chris Martin is one of the few Test cricketers who have taken more wickets than they have scored runs. Can you confirm this and tell me who the other members of this distinguished club may be? **Mo (Canterbury, UK)**

BEARDERS' ANSWER: Chris Martin's tally of wickets certainly does exceed his batting aggregate. Given a qualification of ten Test matches and a minimum of ten wickets, he is the lone Kiwi in an unhappy band of 13. The full list by country is: England – W.E. Bowes (15 Tests, 28 runs, 68 wickets), K. Farnes (15, 58, 60), W.E. Hollies (13, 37, 44), I.J. Jones (15, 38, 44), J.D.F. Larter (10, 16, 37), R. Tattersall (16, 50, 58); Australia – H. Ironmonger (14, 42, 74), B.A. Reid (27, 93, 113), J.V. Saunders (14, 39, 79); South Africa – C.N. McCarthy (15, 28, 36); New Zealand – C.S. Martin (43, 74, 140); India – B.S. Chandrasekhar (58, 167, 242), N.D. Hirwani (17, 54, 66).

Q Earlier this season there were no extras when Sussex scored 203 in the first innings of their County Championship match against Somerset at Taunton. What is the highest First-Class or Test innings without an extra? **Mark Sells (Taunton)**

BEARDERS' ANSWER: The highest Test innings without an extra is 328 by Pakistan in the Third Test against India at Bagh-i-Jinnah, Lahore, on 29–30 January 1955. Philip Bailey has confirmed that the First-Class record (and the only instance over 500) is nearly double that – 647 by Victoria v Tasmania at Melbourne on 5–6 February 1952.

Q I can't help noticing that many of the records for low-scoring Test matches seem to date back to early days (nineteenth century/early twentieth). The distinct impression is that batsmen were weaker then (or bowlers stronger). What was the highest aggregate match score before the First World War? How does it compare to the current record? **Steve, Northampton**

BEARDERS' ANSWER: A poor standard of pitches contributed to low scoring in many of those pre-1914 Test matches. For the record, the highest match aggregate in that period was 1,646 runs for 40 wickets by Australia (465 and 339) and South Africa (482 and 360) in a timeless Test at Adelaide in 1910–1911 that lasted six days.

The current record (1,981 runs for 35 wickets) has stood since March 1939 when South Africa (530 and 481) and England (316 and 645-5) contested a ten-day match that ended in a draw when the tourists had to catch their transport home.

Q I love the column. I was just wondering what is the most wickets to fall on the first day of a Test match. And on any day? **Josh (London)**

BEARDERS' ANSWER: The most wickets to fall on any day of Test cricket is 27 on the second day at Lord's in 1888. Heavy overnight rain prevented the match from starting until 3pm on 16 July, Australia being dismissed for 116 before reducing England to 18-3 by stumps. Next day, on an uncovered pitch reduced to drying mud, England lost their last seven wickets for 35, bowled out Australia for 60 and were themselves routed for 62 to lose by 61 runs at 4.25pm. The aggregate of 291 remained the lowest in a completed Test match until 1931–1932.

The second-highest number of wickets to fall in a single day, and the record for any first day, is 25 by Australia (112 and 48-5) against England (61 – in 68 minutes) on a rain-affected pitch at Melbourne on 1 January 1902.

Q I used to play at Chalkwell Park for Westcliff and, subsequently, for Leigh-on-Sea. I remember that the Australians were rumoured to have played there and scored a record amount of runs in one day. I have tried to use Google but to no avail. Could you confirm if this myth is true? If so, is it still the record for the most runs scored by a team in one day? **Dannymagix**

BEARDERS' ANSWER: The 1948 Australians did score a record 721 runs off 129 overs against Essex on 15 May 1948. Bill Brown (153), Don Bradman (187), Sam Loxton (120) and Ron Saggers (104) were the main contributors before the last five wickets fell for 57 runs. With Trevor Bailey injured and unable to bat, Essex were dismissed for 83 and 187 on the second day to lose by an innings and 451 runs. However, that match was not played at Westcliff. It took place a five-minute drive along the coast in Southchurch Park at Southend-on-Sea.

The Australians' 721 does indeed remain the highest score by one team in a single day of First-Class cricket.

Q Mark Ramprakash has just scored 490 runs across consecutive innings in multiple matches before losing his wicket. Who and what are the records for this in Tests and First-Class cricket? Is over 500 commonplace or as exceptional as I'd imagine? **Iain**

BEARDERS' ANSWER: No batsman has scored 500 runs between dismissals in Test match cricket and only eight have managed 400 or more. Sachin Tendulkar holds the record with 497 for India in four innings in 2003–2004: 241* and 60* v Australia (Sydney), 194* v Pakistan (Multan) and 2 v Pakistan (Lahore).

The First-Class record is 709 (218*, 36*, 234*, 77* and 144) by K.C. Ibrahim for Bombay in 1947–1948.

Three others (G.A. Hick 645, V.M. Merchant 634 and E.H. Hendren 630) have enjoyed an unbroken runs sequence of 600 or more.

In 1994, J.D. Carr (Middlesex) ended the season by scoring 854 runs for once out: 78*, 171*, 136, 106*, 40*, 62* and 261*.

Q I was wondering about very low Test batting averages. Does Chris Martin (NZ) have the worst average ever? The other candidates I could think of (Courtney Walsh, Danish Kaneria, Phil Tufnell, Alan Mullally, Bob Holland and Bert Ironmonger) all seem to have marginally better figures. **Stephen G. Jones, Hampshire**

BEARDERS' ANSWER: Given a qualification of 20 innings there are four batsmen who have averaged under 3.00 in Test cricket. Martin is in third place:

M. Mbangwa, Zimbabwe (1996–2000): 25 innings, 34 runs at an average of 2.00
J.V. Saunders, Australia (1902–1908): 23 innings, 39 runs at an average of 2.29
C.S. Martin, New Zealand (2000–2008): 61 innings, 74 runs at an average of 2.39
H. Ironmonger, Australia (1928–1933): 21 innings, 42 runs at an average of 2.63

The Second Test between West Indies and Sri Lanka at Port-of-Spain in April produced innings scores of 278, 294, 268 and 254 for 4. Would this be the narrowest range of innings scores in a completed match (i.e. 40 runs between the highest and lowest innings scores within the game)? **Barry**

BEARDERS' ANSWER: No, it certainly is not. The smallest range is just 10 runs. That occurred in a match when all 40 wickets fell (and which I was fortunate enough to be scoring for the BBC), on 26–30 December 1982: England 284 and 294; Australia 287 and 288. This Test, the 250th between Australia and England, provided the first instance of sides being all out at close of play on three consecutive days.

 Who scored the 1,000th century in Test cricket? **Ross Deere, Queensland**

BEARDERS' ANSWER: That was Ian Chappell against West Indies in Australia's first innings of the second Test at Melbourne on 27 December 1968. He just pipped Bill Lawry, who recorded the 1,001st later in the same (final) session of the second day. By coincidence, Chappell was dismissed for 165, the same score on which Charles Bannerman was compelled to retire hurt having completed the very first hundred in the inaugural Test on the same ground in March 1877.

Q The other day I noticed that Robert Key's one and only Test century was converted into a double. Have any other Test cricketers done this? **Phil Hopton**

BEARDERS' ANSWER: Nine others have registered a solitary Test century in excess of 199. Kuruppu and Lloyd failed to reach another fifty. The full list is:

England – R.E. Foster (8 Tests, 14 innings, HS 287), R.W.T. Key (15, 26, 221), D. Lloyd (9, 15, 214*); Australia – J.N. Gillespie (71, 93, 201*), B.J. Hodge (6, 11, 203*); New Zealand – M.P. Donnelly (7, 12, 206); West Indies – S.F.A.F. Bacchus (19, 30, 250), D. St E. Atkinson (22, 35, 219); Pakistan – Taslim Arif (6, 10, 210*); Sri Lanka – D.S.B.P. Kuruppu (4, 7, 201*).

Q Is there a Stats site you can recommend that does not include the farcical Australians v ICC World XI match played in Australia in 2005–2006? Cricinfo insists on including these figures despite the ICC definition of Test matches not being met by the match in question. **Phasla**

BEARDERS' ANSWER: Ric Finlay's Tastats site allows you to exclude all matches involving multinational teams (except West Indies!) from its Test and limited-overs matches. Another Australian, Charlie Wat, compiles and updates Test records excluding that match. You will not find it included in any figures published under my name. Hopefully the ICC will soon see the error of their ways and revoke its phoney status.

Q There is always much discussion about how wicket-keepers hate conceding byes. Has a table of the biggest bye-conceders been produced? Could one produce a keeping average, based on byes conceded divided by the number of dismissals they have taken?
Antony Hopker

BEARDERS' ANSWER: Yes, tables of byes-per-wicket-keeper are available. Mark Boucher, who has made the most dismissals in Tests (447), has also conceded the most byes (771). His average of byes-per-wicket is 1.72. Adam Gilchrist (409 dismissals and 602 byes) has a superior byes-per-wicket average of 1.47.

Q I noticed in the recent Yorkshire v Notts match that Yorkshire had 11 lbws against them in the match. Is this a record number of lbws in a match?
Friarmere111

BEARDERS' ANSWER: It may be. No one has scoured nearly 50,700 First-Class matches to find out.

The Test record is the ten inflicted on New Zealand by Pakistan at Lahore in 1996–1997. The most involving both sides in a Test is 17 (West Indies (8) v Pakistan (9) at Port-of-Spain in 1992–1993). The most in a Test match innings is seven (Zimbabwe v England at Chester-le-Street in 2003 and New Zealand v Australia at Christchurch in 2004–2005).

Q I believe there are a number of instances in Test cricket where all 11 batsmen have scored double figures. Could you please tell me what were the most runs scored by the batsman with the lowest score within the team? **John B (High Wycombe)**

BEARDERS' ANSWER: There have been 11 instances of all 11 scoring at least 10 in a Test innings. The highest score by the lowest contributor to such an innings is 12 by R.G. Nadkarni for India (359) v New Zealand at Dunedin in 1967–1968.

Q Name some cricketers whose career average is higher than their individual highest score in Test matches. **Santonu Borpuzari**

BEARDERS' ANSWER: Given a qualification of ten innings, there are just two players whose batting averages exceeded their highest score. Pakistan's Antao D'Souza (10 inns, 8 not outs, 76 runs, average 38.00), had a highest score of 23 not out. India's S.G. Shinde (11 inns, 5 not outs, 85 runs, average 14.17), just qualified with a highest score of 14.

Q What is the progress of lowest scores for the fall of each wicket? I've read about 0 runs for four wickets, so that progress starts 0, 0, 0 and 0. Has any side ever been 0 for 5, or 0 for 6, at Test match level? **Pete B**

BEARDERS' ANSWER: No. The lowest scores at the fall of each wicket from the fourth wicket onwards are:

4th: 0, India (165) v England, Leeds 1952
5th: 6, India (98) v England, the Oval 1952
6th: 7, Australia (70) v England, Manchester 1888
7th: 14, Australia (44) v England, the Oval 1896
8th: 19, Australia (44) v England, the Oval 1896
9th: 25, Australia (44) v England, the Oval 1896
10th: 26, New Zealand (26) v England, Auckland 1954–1955

Q Is Sydney Barnes's bowling average of 16.43 the lowest among bowlers who have played more than 25 Tests and taken more than 150 wickets? **Prashant**

BEARDERS' ANSWER: Yes, his 189 wickets from 27 Tests at 16.43 apiece cost four fewer runs than his closest challenger, Australia's Alan Davison (44 Tests), who took 186 wickets at 20.53. The only other bowlers to take 150 or more wickets at fewer than 21 runs apiece are the West Indies pace trio of Malcolm Marshall (376 at 20.94), Joel Garner (259 at 20.97) and Curtly Ambrose (405 at 20.99).

Q Please can you explain why, when a batsman is not out at the end of an innings, although his runs count towards his career average, the innings itself is not used as a divisor? Surely this gives a false impression of a batsman's prowess? For example, a number 11 could, in theory, play 100 Test innings, scoring 1 in each. If he was not out in 99 of those innings, his Test average would end up as 100. Surely if each innings was counted as a divisor this would be a truer reflection of the player's ability, as his average would then be 1? I know my example is an extreme case, but it would surely make sense that a player's runs divided by total innings should be the criteria for an average. **Colin Smith**

BEARDERS' ANSWER: Ever since batting averages were introduced, 'not out' innings have been disregarded in the calculations. I agree that it is not logical, but it has been established over two centuries. No one has invented an alternative method to the arithmetic mean for calculating batting and bowling averages. Pioneer cricket statisticians decided that it would be unfair to include not out innings when batsmen had gone to the crease shortly before the innings ended or had been undefeated after a long innings. There have been very few instances where a player's career, tour or season's average has been grossly inflated by 'not outs'. The most famous such instance occurred on the Australians' 1953 tour of England when their number 11, Bill Johnston, achieved a First-Class batting average of 102.00 by virtue of being dismissed only once during his 17 innings and compiling an aggregate of 102 runs with a highest score of 28 not out. Once his average had reached three figures, his captain, Lindsay Hassett, protected it by declaring so that he did not bat again on the tour.

Q I believe there are four or five players who have taken wickets with their first ball in international cricket. Wavell Hinds is one. Who are the others?
Prafull

BEARDERS' ANSWER: There have been many more instances

than that. A total of 13 bowlers have struck gold with their first ball in Test cricket and another 14 have done so in limited-overs internationals. The lists are:

Test matches: A. Coningham (Australia); W.M. Bradley, E.G. Arnold, G.G. Macauley, M.W. Tate, R. Howorth, R.K. Illingworth (England); T.F. Johnson (West Indies); M. Henderson, H.D. Smith (New Zealand); N.M. Kulkarni (India); Intikhab Alam (Pakistan); and M.K.G.C.P. Lakshitha (Sri Lanka).

Internationals: G.G. Arnold, R. Clarke (England); M. van Jaarsveld, M. Zondeki (South Africa); C.H. Lloyd, W.W. Hinds, F.H. Edwards (West Indies); S.A. Thomson (New Zealand); S. Ramesh (India); Shahid Mahboob, Inzamam ul-Haq (Pakistan); K.S. Lokuarachchi (Sri Lanka); E.Z. Matambanadzo (Zimbabwe); J.S. Ababu (Kenya).

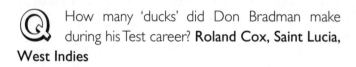 How many 'ducks' did Don Bradman make during his Test career? **Roland Cox, Saint Lucia, West Indies**

BEARDERS' ANSWER: The Don was dismissed for nought in seven of his 80 Test innings, the two in 1936–1937 occurring in successive knocks.

Series	Opponents	Venue	Bowler
1930–1931	West Indies	Sydney	Herman Griffith
1932–1933	England	Melbourne	Bill Bowes

1936–1937	England	Brisbane	Gubby Allen
1936–1937	England	Sydney	Bill Voce
1946–1947	England	Adelaide	Alec Bedser
1948	England	Nottingham	Alec Bedser
1948	England	The Oval	Eric Hollies

Batting Maestros

(Q) Is Graeme Hick the only player to have scored First-Class triple centuries in three different decades? **Paul**

BEARDERS' ANSWER: Intriguing question, Paul. The answer is yes: Graeme Hick (1988, 1997 and 2002) is alone in scoring a First-Class 300 in three separate decades. Don Bradman (6) scored his in the 1920s and 1930s, Bill Ponsford and Wally Hammond (4 each) all in the 1920s and 1930s respectively, W.G. Grace (3) in 1876 (2) and 1896, and Brian Lara (3) in 1994 (2) and 2004.

(Q) Who has scored the most double centuries in all First-Class cricket, and where does Zaheer Abbas figure on the list? Pretty high, I think? **Zainab Vohra, Pakistan**

BEARDERS' ANSWER: Sorry to disappoint you, Zainab,

but Zaheer Abbas (10) is equal 22nd in the list of batsmen scoring most double hundreds. It is headed by Sir Donald Bradman (37) and Walter Hammond (36). The only other batsman with 20 or more scores of 200 is 'Patsy' Hendren (22).

 What is the highest ever Test batting average for a calendar year? **Chris Ziesler**

BEARDERS' ANSWER: Had Kumar Sangakkara scored another 32 runs in 2007, he would have qualified for the list of those who have scored 1,000 runs in a calendar year and would have been only the fourth to do so while averaging three figures. The three he would have joined are Sir Garfield Sobers (1,193 @ 132.55 in 1958), Sir Donald Bradman (1,025 @ 113.88 in 1948), and Ricky Ponting (1,503 @ 100.20 in 2003).

Bill, have here been any cases of Test match 300-run partnerships where one partner did not even manage a 100? **Ashok Iyengar, US**

BEARDERS' ANSWER: There have been three, Ashok:
 303 (3rd wkt) Viv Richards (232) & Alvin Kallicharran (97), WI v E, Nottingham, 1976.
 313 (8th) Wasim Akram (257*) & Saqlain Mushtaq

(79), P v Z, Sheikhupura, 1996–1997.

322 (5th) Brian Lara (213) & Jimmy Adams (94), WI v A, Kingston, 1998–1999.

Q Was Ian Botham's 208 vs India at the Oval in 1982 the fastest ever Test match double century?
Adam Harchuk, England

BEARDERS' ANSWER: In terms of fewest balls received, his 220 is the fastest on record in Test cricket. But scoring methods did not record balls received for many of the early innings.

The fastest 200 in terms of time is 214 minutes by Donald Bradman during his 334 for Australia v England at Leeds in 1934. Botham took 268 minutes.

Q I once carried my bat and was four not out from a total of 34 all out. Is this a record please? **Peter Dann, England**

BEARDERS' ANSWER: I cannot find any Carried Bat records in minor cricket to compare to your feat. However, as instances of sides being bowled out for nought are not infrequent, some opening bat has probably remained not out zero in at least one of them.

The lowest score by anyone carrying their bat through

a First-Class innings is five by R.G. ('Dick') Barlow, the redoubtable Lancashire and England 'stonewaller', who achieved the feat 11 times.

His record five not out, in a total of 69 against Nottinghamshire at Trent Bridge in 1882, occupied two hours.

Q Have there been Tests where four or more players failed in the nervous nineties? **Cathal Boylan, Ireland**

BEARDERS' ANSWER: After considerable research, I can reveal that four batsmen (Robin Smith and Allan Lamb of England, and Dipak Patel and John Wright of New Zealand) were dismissed in the nineties at Lancaster Park, Christchurch, in January 1992. There was a second instance at the Oval in August 1995 when Graeme Hick, 'Jack' Russell and Michael Atherton of England, and Richie Richardson of West Indies were the victims.

At Karachi in March 1973, Majid Khan and Mushtaq Mohammed of Pakistan and Dennis Amiss of England were each dismissed for 99. There have been no fewer than 726 scores of between 90 and 99 inclusive in Test cricket, with Australia and England registering the most, with 151 instances apiece. Steve Waugh (10) has scored most, followed by Rahul Dravid and Michael Slater with nine.

Who was the last England opener to carry his bat? How many times has this happened in England's history? **Alexander, UK**

BEARDERS' ANSWER: Michael Atherton was the last to achieve this feat for England when he batted throughout their first innings of 228 against New Zealand at Christchurch on 15–16 February 1997. His undefeated 94 took 346 minutes and came from 235 balls with 10 fours.

His was the eighth instance by an England opener, the others involving Bobby Abel (1891–1892), Pelham Warner (1898–1899), Len Hutton (1950 and 1950–1951), Geoffrey Boycott (1979–1980), Graham Gooch (1991) and Alec Stewart (1992).

Have any pair of brothers both made hundreds in each innings of a Test match? **TJ, Australia**

BEARDERS' ANSWER: Ian (145 and 121) and Greg Chappell (247* and 133) for Australia v New Zealand at Wellington in March 1974.

R.E. and W.L. Foster (Worcestershire v Hampshire at Worcester in 1899) are the only other pair of brothers to achieve this feat in First-Class cricket.

Q I know that Shane Warne has scored the most Test runs (3,142) without ever getting a century (his nearest challengers, Vaas and Kumble, both got centuries recently), but which batsman has scored the most runs without ever getting a fifty? **Jonathan Ellis**

BEARDERS' ANSWER: Waqar Younis is your man. He scored 1,010 runs, average 10.20, in 120 innings, with a top score of 45. His nearest challenger is Fred Trueman with 981 runs, average 13.82, from 85 innings and a highest score of only 39 not out.

Q Andrew Symonds scored eight runs from one ball against New Zealand (an all-run four followed by four overthrows). Is this the record for the number of runs from a legitimate delivery in a Test?

Also, can you get any more than four overthrows? **Jon**

BEARDERS' ANSWER: There is no limit to the number of overthrows that can be run from a single delivery.

Eight could well be the Test record for the most runs scored off one ball. Seven is the most I have recorded in the 375 Tests I have scored to date. That instance occurred during the fourth West Indies Test at Headingley in 1976 when Alan Knott took a quick single to extra-cover where Bernard Julien fielded and overthrew the wicket-keeper. The batsmen ran two overthrows before Andy Roberts at square-leg retrieved the ball. His throw eluded the stumps at the bowler's end and crossed the long-off boundary.

The most in First-Class cricket is 10 by S.H. Wood for Derbyshire v MCC at Lord's in 1900. There have been 14 recorded instances of nine, the most recent, also at Lord's, in 1949.

 Do you know what is the highest score made by a team in which no player scored more than 50?
Andrew Ward, UK

BEARDERS' ANSWER: Good one, Andrew. I am assuming you mean 'in which no player scored more than 49'. I haven't time to check the scorecards of all 1,546 Test matches, but I can offer 258 by Australia v England at Edgbaston in 1981 when the highest individual score was 47 by their captain, Kim Hughes.

That match was the second of only two completed Tests in which no batsman scored a fifty, Mike Brearley's 48 being the top score. The first instance occurred in January 1935 when England beat West Indies on a rain-affected pitch in Barbados.

PS. While researching my answer to a later question, I discovered four higher totals in a list in *'Mosts without'* *In Test Cricket* by Keith Walmsley, who is currently the Cricket Society's statistician. The correct answer to your question is 302 and the full list of totals of 250 and over without an individual fifty is:

302 SA v NZ Wellington 1963–1964
265-8d E v I Manchester 1959
262-7 NZ v P Karachi 1976–1977
259 A v E Melbourne 1876–1877
258 I v WI Bridgetown 1961–1962
258 A v E Birmingham 1981
253 E v NZ Christchurch 1962–1963

Q I remember reading in the mid 1980s that David Gower – rather surprisingly for a player of such sublime yet wayward brilliance – held the record for the longest run of Test innings without a duck. The figure, I recall, was 99 innings.

Is this true and, if so, does the record still stand? **Ben Dowell, UK**

BEARDERS' ANSWER: David Gower extended that sequence to 119 consecutive innings without a duck. He made six noughts in his first 73 innings (44 Tests between 1978 and 1982) but none in his next 66 matches. His only other nought came in the second innings at Melbourne in 1990–1991 when England were chasing quick runs for victory.

The next longest sequence of duckless innings is 96 by Richie Richardson for West Indies between 1984–1985 and 1991.

Q Allan Border once had scores of 98 not out and 100 in the same Test against West Indies. Is this the only instance of a batsman scoring a hundred and remaining unbeaten in the 1990s in the same Test?
Prashant, New York

BEARDERS' ANSWER: Border (at Port-of-Spain in 1983–1984) is the only Australian to do this, but four other batsmen (two apiece from England and West Indies) have achieved this unusual double: Gary Sobers (Georgetown 1967–1968), Mike Atherton (Christchurch 1996–1997), Shiv Chanderpaul (Lord's 2004) and Andrew Strauss (Port Elizabeth 2004–2005).

Q Andy Flower scored 341 runs in the first Test v South Africa – and still lost. Is this the highest number of runs made in a losing side and, if so, who held the previous record? **Matt Blakeley, New Zealand**

BEARDERS' ANSWER: Excellent question, Matt. Yes, Flower's 341 is the highest Test match aggregate by a batsman on the losing side. It beat a 'record' that had stood for more than 76 years when, at Melbourne in January 1925, Yorkshire's Herbert Sutcliffe scored 176 and 127 (303) but was unable to prevent Australia from winning by 81 runs. A timeless Test, it lasted seven days.

Sutcliffe was the first to score hundreds in both innings against Australia.

 Who scored the most runs in Test cricket in a calendar year? **Mark, USA**

BEARDERS' ANSWER: Mohammad Yousuf Youhana holds that record with 1,788 runs, average 99.33, including nine centuries in 19 innings for Pakistan in 2006.

 I recently set a quiz question, based on information from a website: Is Neil Fairbrother the only batsman to have scored a century in each session of a First-Class match (366 for Lancashire v Surrey at the Oval a few years ago)? Somebody thought that Bradman had also achieved this. **Tony Phillips, England**

BEARDERS' ANSWER: During his 366 against Surrey in 1990 Neil Fairbrother did indeed score 100 or more in each session: 100 off 102 balls, 108 from 109 and 103 from 110 – 311 in the day. I'm not aware of any other batsman achieving this feat.

Contrary to statements in some publications, Sir Donald Bradman did NOT score a hundred in each session during his 334 at Headingley in 1930. His session scores were 105, 115 and 89.

Q What is the highest number of runs scored in an innings by a batsman while using a runner?
harry8611

BEARDERS' ANSWER: There have been at least 30 instances of batsmen scoring hundreds in First-Class cricket using a runner for a major part of their innings, 12 of them throughout its entirety. The first was by Alfred Mynn, who scored 125 not out for the South v the North at Leicester in 1836. He injured his leg during pre-match practice, and it became sufficiently serious for amputation to be considered. He didn't play again until 1838.

Scores where a runner was summoned in mid-innings are not available in many cases. The highest number of runs in a single innings made with a runner that I have on record is 155 by Paul Prichard during his 224 for Essex v Kent at Canterbury in 1997. He acquired a runner after scoring 69. The highest complete innings with a runner is 150 not out by D.J. (Danny) Buckingham for Tasmania v Western Australia at Perth in 1986–1987.

The only batsman to score two complete hundreds in a match with the aid of a runner is Graeme Fowler of Lancashire, Durham, England and *Test Match Special*. Playing for Lancashire at Southport in 1982, he strained his thigh while fielding on the first day during Warwickshire's innings of 523-4 declared, but batted without a runner to score 26 not out at stumps. He then scored exactly 100 before lunch on the second day with David Lloyd as his runner. In the second innings, Ian Folley ran for him (and acknowledged the crowd's applause for the century) when 'Foxy' scored 128 not out on the third day.

Q Iain O'Brien's 38-ball duck in a partnership of 50 in Adelaide must be some sort of superlative but may have been beaten. When and by whom? **RobinP63**

BEARDERS' ANSWER: It may well be the first 50 partnership in which one partner failed to score, but preparations for a probable departure to India allow scant time for research. The nearest I have spotted is Shahadat Hossain's contribution of 3 not out to a tenth-wicket stand of 69 with Mohammad Rafique for Bangladesh against Australia at Chittagong in 2005–2006.

The longest duck in Test cricket took 101 minutes (77 balls) and was the work of New Zealand's Geoff Allott against South Africa at Auckland in 1998–1999, but his last-wicket stand with Chris Harris added only 32.

Q We heard throughout the 2001 Ashes series how many times Mike Atherton was dismissed by Glenn McGrath. But in all of their meetings, how many runs has Atherton scored off McGrath? Surely, the contest can't have been so one-sided as the 19 dismissals might suggest? **Tim Hardman, UK**

BEARDERS' ANSWER: McGrath dismissed Atherton in 19 of the 34 innings in which he bowled against him between 1994–1995 and last season. As I scored all the 17 Test matches in question, I am probably in a unique position to supply the answer but sadly not in time to meet my deadline for this batch of questions. However, I will have the aggregate for you in the next batch so your question will gain a second billing!

… Tim, as promised I have now researched a full answer to your very interesting question.

McGrath dismissed Atherton in 19 of the 34 innings in which he bowled against him between 1994–1995 and last season. Combing my scoresheets of all the 17 Test matches in question, I can reveal that Atherton scored a total of 677 runs in those 34 innings, 248 of them (including 40 fours and a five) off 628 balls from McGrath (39.49 runs/100 balls). The most he scored in any innings off McGrath was 24 (out of 57 not out) off 15 balls at Edgbaston when England won in 1997.

Divided by those 19 dismissals gives him an average of 13.05 runs/wicket against his chief adversary. His overall Test average was 37.70. For his 66 innings in 33 Tests against Australia it dropped to 29.69.

Q Is Ian Ward the first specialist opener to have batted as low as number eight while not being injured? **Mark & Phill, NZ**

BEARDERS' ANSWER: Very good question. The answer is 'No'. Len Hutton batted No. 8 in England's second innings against Australia at Brisbane in 1950–1951 as a ploy to counteract the effects of a 'sticky', rain-affected pitch. He played a remarkable unbeaten innings of 62 out of a total of 122. Denis Compton batted at No. 9. There are probably other instances in 1,547 Test matches, but this one answers your question.

Q Has there ever been an instance of a Test cricketer not registering a single duck in their entire career? **Andrew Haine, UK**

BEARDERS' ANSWER: If we restrict the list to those playing a minimum of 20 innings in Tests, there have been 21 players who were never dismissed without scoring. That list is headed by two Australians, Jim W. Burke (44 innings) and 'Reggie' A. Duff (40).

The longest duckless career for England is 27 innings by Walter W. Read, who is 11th on the overall list.

Q How many people have matched Mark Ramprakash's achievement of averaging over 100 in First-Class cricket in two separate seasons? **Alison B**

BEARDERS' ANSWER: Only one, Alison. Geoff Boycott averaged 100.12 in 1971 and 102.53 in 1979. Mark is alone in achieving this feat in successive seasons.

Three other batsmen and one tail ender have averaged 100: Don Bradman (115.66 in 1938); Damien Martyn (104.66 in 2001), Graham Gooch (101.70 in 1990); and the fluke, Bill Johnston (102.00 by being out only once in 17 innings in 1953).

Q What is the lowest score made by a team winning a Test match by an innings – batting first and second? **sirianblog**

BEARDERS' ANSWER: Both those lowest innings-winning totals were made on vicious 'sticky' pitches as they dried after heavy rain.

The lowest such first-innings score is 172 by England against Australia (81 and 70) at Manchester in 1888 when a record 18 (Australian) wickets fell before lunch on the second day in the shortest completed Test match in England – 6 hours 34 minutes. The tourists were compelled to follow on as the margin in 1888 was a mere 80 runs.

Australia's 153 against South Africa (36 and 45) at Melbourne in 1931–1932 is the lowest to gain an innings victory batting second.

Q Australia recently scored 569 in a county fixture with no batsman scoring a hundred. Is this the highest First-Class total not to contain a century? **Sanjeev Zumkhawala, UK**

BEARDERS' ANSWER: It may well be, but it would take many hours of research to check all the higher innings to make sure. The highest Test innings without a hundred is 524-9d by India against New Zealand at Kanpur in 1976–1977.

Q My question comes from the fact that my team has often had low totals where 'extras' has been the highest scorer. What is the highest score in a Test innings where extras have outscored the batsmen? I doubt we'd ever beat it, but it would be interesting to know as a target! **Andy (York)**

BEARDERS' ANSWER: Your target to beat is 58, Andy. Extras have been the highest contributor to a Test match innings on 13 occasions, the most recent being in England's first innings against West Indies at Kingston,

Jamaica, in March 2004. England's total (339), the number of extras (60) and the highest individual score (58) are each the highest tallies when extras have top scored.

 The West Indies recently defended a ridiculously low total against Zimbabwe, and England, of course, defended 130 against Australia in 1981. But what is the lowest fourth-innings total that has been defended?
John, Australia

BEARDERS' ANSWER: The lowest defended target is 85 by Australia (who dismissed England for 77) at the Oval in 1882. 'The Demon' Spofforth took 7 for 44 (14 wickets in the match) and the *Sporting Times* carried a mock obituary notice which led to the birth of the Ashes.

During the final tense stages of this match, one spectator died of heart failure and another bit through his umbrella handle. The West Indies v Zimbabwe match at Port-of-Spain in 1999–2000 provided the second-lowest defended target, Zimbabwe being dismissed for 63 when they required 99.

Has a Test team ever lost by an innings in every match of a Test series? If not, what's the record for most innings defeats by one side in a series? **Jason Crawley, England**

BEARDERS' ANSWER: Yes, there have been two instances of a side gaining innings victories in each match of a three-Test rubber.

England beat West Indies by an innings in each of their matches at Lord's, Old Trafford and the Oval in 1928. India beat Sri Lanka by an innings in each of their matches at Lucknow, Bangalore and Ahmedabad in 1993–1994. This feat completed a sequence of six successive home victories by innings margins for India.

Has a team ever lost all wickets in both innings of a Test by the same method (e.g. all bowled or all lbw)? **Richard Powell, England**

BEARDERS' ANSWER: No. The closest instance occurred at the Gabba, Brisbane, in 1982–1983 when Australia caught all ten England wickets in the first innings and nine in the second.

I have heard of a cricket match where the batting team was bowled out for nothing. When they came out to field, the first ball was a no-ball so the game was over. Do you know if this is true and when and where it occurred? **Gideon Reed, Great Britain**

BEARDERS' ANSWER: Yes, I remember reading about it many years ago, but I don't have the details.

Up to 1897, when A.L. Ford's *Curiosities of Cricket* was published (as a limited edition of 25 copies), there had been 18 instances of sides being dismissed for 0. I haven't seen an updated list – a project for the Association of Cricket Statisticians and Historians, perhaps?

 Has any side ever scored more than 1,000 runs in a single innings? **Peter, England**

BEARDERS' ANSWER: Yes, it has happened twice in First-Class cricket, both instances occurring in Australia during timeless matches and being amassed by Victoria on their home ground in Melbourne: 1,107 v New South Wales in 633 minutes on 24 and 27 December 1927, and 1,059 v Tasmania in 641 minutes on 2, 3, 5 February 1923. Melbourne, but not the MCG, was also the scene of a total of 1,094 by Melbourne University v Essendon in 1897–1898.

Q The first seven Sri Lanka A batsman scored 50 or more during their innings of 749-5 declared against South Africa A in an unofficial Test at Potchefstroom.

What is the record for most players scoring fifties in a single innings? Is this a record for the most consecutive players in the batting order registering one? **Alex, UK via Brisbane**

BEARDERS' ANSWER: The most fifties in a First-Class innings is eight by the 1893 Australians against Oxford & Cambridge Past & Present at Portsmouth but they were not scored by the first eight batsmen.

The Test record is seven, and there have been three instances: England v Australia at Manchester in 1934; Pakistan v India at Karachi in 2005–2006; and Sri Lanka v England at Lord's in 2006. The second instance, involving Pakistan, was achieved by the first seven batsmen. So the recent Sri Lanka A performance was one short of the First-Class record but equalled the one involving consecutive batsmen.

Q What is the highest second-innings score recorded by a Test team that has followed on? **Barrie Street (Canada)**

BEARDERS' ANSWER: Having mustered only 171 in their first innings in reply to Australia's 445 at Calcutta in

2000–2001, India claimed that record by amassing 657 for 7 declared. They then dismissed the visitors for 212 to gain a 171-run victory – only the third by a side following-on in Tests.

Bowling Wizards

Q Last season I took five wickets in five balls. We called Wisden to see if anybody else had done this at any level of cricket; apparently somebody in Yorkshire has. My question is, has this ever been achieved in the First-Class echelons? **Michael Lovelady, England**

BEARDERS' ANSWER: The Demon Lovelady! Well bowled!

No bowler has taken more than four wickets with successive balls in First-Class cricket. The nearest is the feat of C.W.L. (Charlie) Parker, who hit the stumps five times in consecutive balls in his benefit match for Gloucestershire v Yorkshire at Bristol in 1922, but the second was a no-ball.

There are two instances in school/college cricket of bowlers taking nine wickets with successive balls: Paul Hugo for Smithfield School v Aliwal North in South Africa in February 1931; and Stephen Fleming (not the NZ captain) for Marlborough College 'A' XI v Bohally Intermediate at Blenheim, New Zealand in December 1967.

I once sat in the Lillee-Marsh Stand at the WACA ground in Perth and watched Curtly Ambrose bowl an 18-ball over versus Australia. Is this the longest over bowled in Test cricket? **Dave Whitely, UK**

BEARDERS' ANSWER: Ambrose played in three Perth Tests, and I eventually tracked down the over you witnessed. According to the excellent *Allan's Australian Cricket Annual* it was a 15-ball over (not 18), containing 9 no-balls and it took 12 minutes to bowl. Allan Miller describes it as 'perhaps the longest over in Test cricket'.

In terms of balls bowled, I have no record of a longer one, but such things have not always been noted in match reports and only a detailed examination of the score sheets of all Test innings would produce a definitive table. The closest I have on record is the 13-ball over (3 wides, 4 no-balls) delivered by G.O.B. 'Gubby' Allen v Australia at Old Trafford in 1934.

What is the most consecutive maidens bowled by anyone? **James**

BEARDERS' ANSWER: The record for six-ball overs in both Test and First-Class cricket is 21 by R.G. ('Bapu') Nadkarni for India against England at Madras in January 1964. A left-handed slow bowler, he could command an immaculate length and returned the astonishing analysis of 32 overs, 27 maidens, 5 runs and 0 wickets in the first innings when several of the England players were suffering from severe stomach problems. His sequence of 131 balls without conceding a run has been surpassed only by South African off-spinner Hugh Tayfield, who bowled 137 balls, including 16 eight-ball maidens, spread over both innings, against England at Durban in January 1957.

 How many Test wickets did 'Beefy' get in his Test career? **William Boyle, England, Norfolk**

BEARDERS' ANSWER: I assume you are referring to Ian Botham. He took 383 wickets in 102 Tests, 58 more than any other England bowler, including five in an innings 27 times and ten in a match four times. His breakdown of wickets against each country was: 148 v Australia; 64 v New Zealand; 61 v West Indies; 59 v India; 40 v Pakistan and 11 v Sri Lanka.

As a young bloke at Melville Cricket Club in Western Australia, I had a bowling coach by the name of D.K. Lillee. Everyone knows him as FOT but the exact origin of this nickname is unknown. Any clues? **Dave Johnstone, Netherlands**

BEARDERS' ANSWER: G.A.R. 'Tony' Lock inadvertently

gave him the nickname 'FOT' when he was captain of WA in one of Lillee's early Sheffield Shield matches.

Unimpressed with Lillee's efforts that day, he admonished his young speedster with: 'Lillee! You are bowling like a F***ing Old Tart!'

Q When people speak of 'reverse swing', I only ever hear about bowlers swinging the ball from an outswing action going into the batsmen. Do bowlers ever reverse swing a ball so it leaves the right-handed batsman? If so, who is the best known exponent of it? **Matthew Blackmore, England**

BEARDERS' ANSWER: The only bowler I have heard of who bowls reverse outswing is Shane Bond. He discussed this in an interview after taking six wickets for New Zealand against Australia in the Super Six stage of the current World Cup.

As he admitted he had no idea why it happened, what chance has the bewildered batsman got of predicting it?

Q When was the option of taking the new ball after 80 overs introduced in Tests? What is the largest number of overs that a side has continued with the old ball? **Marcus (UK)**

BEARDERS' ANSWER: Playing conditions governing the availability of a new ball have varied considerably ever since the Second World War. The Ashes series of 1948 was played under an experimental law that allowed a new ball after only 55 overs. The limit had risen to 85 overs when I began my stint with *Test Match Special* in 1966. A lengthy trawl of my scoresheets has revealed that the 80-over edict was introduced in 1996.

The highest recorded number of overs for which the original ball has been retained in Test cricket is 177. Bereft of the services of two of his key bowlers (Malcolm Marshall and Michael Holding) and hampered by one of Wellington's notorious northerly winds in February 1987, West Indies captain Viv Richards countered with this tactic throughout New Zealand's second innings as they amassed 386 for five.

Q As a Middlesex Young Amateur in 1960, I was privileged to take 6 for 14 in 14 overs at Lord's. For the benefit of my ego, how does this compare with best analysis by any bowler at Lord's? **Robin Warren, UK**

BEARDERS' ANSWER: Sadly for your ego, Robin, it scarcely rates a mention!

In First-Class matches alone on the main ground (one was played on the Nursery Ground in 1903), there have been eight instances of bowlers taking ten wickets in an innings.

In addition, there have been 39 nine-wicket hauls and 210 eight-wicket ones.

Q What is the maximum number of wickets taken in one over in a Test match? **Eve Randell, England**

BEARDERS' ANSWER: Four is the record in Test cricket and there have been six instances, half of them at Headingley: M.J.C. Allom for England v New Zealand at Christchurch in 1929–1930; K. Cranston for England v South Africa at Headingley in 1947; F.J. Titmus for England v New Zealand at Headingley in 1965; C.M. Old for England v Pakistan at Edgbaston in 1978; Wasim Akram for Pakistan v West Indies at Lahore in 1990–1991; A.R. Caddick for England v West Indies at Headingley in 2000.

Q In the recent Fourth Test between India and Australia, Jason Krejza went for 358 runs in the match – this can't be far off being a record! **SlowFatMikey**

BEARDERS' ANSWER: Krejza's tally is the runner-up. Only West Indian leg-break bowler O.C. ('Tommy') Scott, with match figures of 9 for 374 at Kingston in 1929–

1930, has conceded more. The bulk of those runs were scored off him in the first innings when he returned the remarkable figures of 80.2 overs, 13 maidens, 266 runs and 5 wickets as England amassed 849 runs at the start of a timeless Test. Andy Sandham was chiefly responsible as he posted the first international triple century in what turned out to be his final Test.

Q In their Fourth Test of the 1970–1971 series (Sunil Gavaskar's debut series) against India at Bridgetown, West Indies employed ten bowlers in the second innings. Has there been an instance where everyone including the wicketkeeper has bowled? How often have ten or more bowlers bowled in a Test innings?
Pbhawalkar

BEARDERS' ANSWER: There have been four instances of all eleven bowling in a Test match and fourteen of ten bowlers being called upon – including seven since the one you mention.

The four involving the entire team were: England v Australia (551), the Oval, 1884; Australia v Pakistan (382-2), Faisalabad, 1979–80; India v West Indies (629-9 dec), St John's, 2001–2002; and South Africa v West Indies (747), St John's, 2004–2005.

Q Who had a better strike-rate after the first 30 Tests of their careers, Sydney Barnes or Waqar Younis? **Orlando, Canada**

BEARDERS' ANSWER: Trick questions are always fun.

S.F. Barnes played in only 27 Tests, during which he took 189 wickets from 7,873 balls at an average rate of 41.65 balls per wicket. After a similar number of Tests (27 of his eventual tally of 87), Waqar Younis had taken 154 wickets from 5,521 balls, a rate of 35.85. After 30 Tests, Waqar's figures were 169 wickets, 6,219 balls, 36.79 rate. His final figures were 373 wickets. 16,224 balls, 43.49 rate.

Q Has a bowler ever doubled as a fast bowler and also a spinner? Is it allowed for a bowler to change bowling style within an over and, if so, does this require notice to the batsman? **Simon**

BEARDERS' ANSWER: The obvious answer to your first question, Simon, is Sir Garfield Sobers who frequently exhibited three types of bowling in the same innings, sometimes within the same spell. After opening with left-arm fast-medium late swing, he would revert to his original left-arm spin, bowling both orthodox leg-breaks and wrist spin (chinamen and googlies).

Bowlers only have to advise a batsman (via the umpire) if they are changing their bowling arm. Changes of style are for the batsman to decipher unaided.

Q In the first [2008] Test match v South Africa, Monty Panesar bowled sixty overs without a wicket. What is the record number of overs bowled in a Test innings without taking a wicket? **Friarmere111**

BEARDERS' ANSWER: The Barbadian off-spinner Denis Atkinson bowled the most wicketless overs in a Test innings – 72 (72-29-137-0) for West Indies v England at Birmingham in 1957. Panesar's 60 fruitless overs ranks equal-ninth in the list, with three England bowlers above him: Jack Young (48 eight-ball overs, the equivalent of 64 six-ball ones) v South Africa at Port Elizabeth in 1948–1949; Maurice Tate (62 v Australia at Melbourne in 1928–1929); and John Emburey (61 v Pakistan at the Oval in 1987).

Q I am interested in the phenomenon of bowlers running out the non-striker while he's backing up. I think it is called 'Mankading'. How many times has this happened in Test cricket? Does the ball count as having been bowled? Is there some reason that this practice is considered poor form? **Larry (Leeds)**

BEARDERS' ANSWER: India's outstanding all-rounder,

'Vinoo' Mankad, was the first of four bowlers to run out a non-striking batsman for backing up before he had bowled the ball in Test cricket. His victim at Sydney in 1947–1948 was Australia's Bill Brown, and Mankad had successfully rehearsed this unusual dismissal against the same batsman at the same venue when the tourists played an Australian XI there a month earlier. Mankad had also warned Brown when he had backed up in their next match against Queensland.

The subsequent three Test match instances involved Ian Redpath (Australia) by Charlie Griffith (West Indies) at Adelaide in 1968–1969, Derek Randall (England) by Ewen Chatfield (New Zealand) at Christchurch in 1978–1979, and Sikander Bakht (Pakistan) by Alan Hurst (Australia) at Perth in 1978–1979.

The ball doesn't count because it hasn't been bowled! It's only bad form if the bowler hasn't previously warned the batsman – who is stealing a run. Law 42, note 15, now permits the bowler to attempt to run out the non-striker only before entering his delivery stride.

 What is a chinaman bowler? **JMB, England**

BEARDERS' ANSWER: A left-handed slow bowler who bowls off-breaks to right-handed batsmen. The first exponent at international level was Ellis Achong, a Trinidadian of Chinese extraction, who played six Tests for West Indies between 1929–30 and 1934–1935.

Which bowler has the highest number of caught and bowleds at Test level? **Marc, England**

BEARDERS' ANSWER: A question that Derek Underwood once asked me, and you will soon know why!

Anil Kumble has the most with 27 of his 547 wickets taken to catches off his own bowling (4.9%) in international Tests.

Of the three other bowlers who have taken 20 or more caught and bowleds, Underwood, with 20 of his 297 wickets, has taken the highest percentage of his wickets in this way (6.7). The other two bowlers are Muthiah Muralitharan with 25 out of 669 (3.7%) and Shane Warne with 21 out of 702 (2.9%).

 Was Doshi the first bowler in the Twenty20 Cup to take a hat-trick and end up on the losing side? Also the commentators referred to a few shots as 'French Cuts'. What does that mean? **Dave, Newcastle**

BEARDERS' ANSWER: Yes, Nayan Doshi was the first. The five previous hat-tricks in this competition (by A.D. Mascarenhas, D.G. Cork, J.E. Anyon, J.N. Snape and R. McLaren) had all contributed to wins.

A French Cut is a false stroke. Also known as a Harrow Drive, Chinese Cut or Surrey Cut, it is an attempted cut or drive that has resulted in the ball travelling to fine leg via an inside or under edge.

Q Shaun Pollock became the 11th bowler to bowl 1,000 maidens in Test cricket. Who were the previous 10? **David Gladstone, UK**

BEARDERS' ANSWER: At the end of 2004, the full list of bowlers with 1,000 maiden overs in Test cricket was: S.K. Warne (Australia – 1,540 maidens/119 Tests), M. Muralitharan (Sri Lanka – 1,381/91), Lance Gibbs (West Indies – 1,313/79), D.L. Underwood (England – 1,239/86), G.D. McGrath (Australia – 1,235/105), A. Kumble (India – 1,195/92), C.A. Walsh (West Indies – 1,145/132), B.S. Bedi (India – 1,096/67), Kapil Dev (India – 1,060/131), S.M. Pollock (South Africa – 1,042/89) and C.E.L. Ambrose (West Indies – 1,000/98).

Prior to 1983–1984 maiden overs were easier to achieve because no-balls and wides were not debited to bowlers' analyses.

Q Who was the last English Test spin bowler to take 100 or more Test wickets at an average of below 30? I bet you have to go back a long way. My guess is Ray Illingworth. **Stephen Joyce, UK**

BEARDERS' ANSWER: Ray Illingworth does not meet your qualification, as his 122 Test wickets cost 31.20 apiece.

Derek Underwood is the most recent (297 wickets

at 25.83). He took his 100th wicket during his 23rd Test (v NZ, Auckland, 1970–1971) and made his final appearance in 1981–1982 v Sri Lanka at Colombo.

Prior to Underwood you have to go back to Tony Lock, whose career ended in 1967–1968.

Q This season, two bowlers took four wickets in four balls on my team's ground. Has there ever been an occurrence of four wickets in four balls taking place twice in a season or even twice on one ground? **Thomas**

BEARDERS' ANSWER: In First-Class matches there have been 35 instances of bowlers taking four wickets with consecutive balls. Bob Crisp (Rhodesia, Western Province, Worcestershire and South Africa) is the only bowler to perform this feat twice. He is also the only Test cricketer to climb Mount Kilimanjaro twice.

Four seasons (1895, 1907, 1914 and 1965–1966) produced two instances, but none involved the same ground. Lord's has been the venue on three occasions, while six other grounds have witnessed two.

Q How do the methods of dismissal of [Test spin bowlers] Muralitharan, Warne and Kumble differ from each other? **Sirianblog**

BEARDERS' ANSWER: Before Murali's appearances in the [2008] Bangladesh v Sri Lanka series, their dismissals were as follows:

Tests	Wickets	B	Ct	LBW	St	Hit	Wkt
Muralitharan	122	751	160	403	143	44	1
Warne	145	708	116	418	138	36	0
Kumble	132	619	94	345	156	24	0

 What is the least number of bowlers used in a completed Test match? **Ian S, UK**

BEARDERS' ANSWER: The fewest I can find is six, three by each side in the Old Trafford Ashes Test of 1888, when England (172) beat Australia (81 and 70) by an innings and 21 runs. The six bowlers were R. Peel, G.A. Lohmann and J. Briggs (England), and J.J. Ferris, C.T.B. Turner and S.M.J. Woods (Australia).

 If 15 overs are taken as a minimum requirement, are there any bowlers who have conceded 0 runs in a Test match innings? If not, who has the most economical figures? **Eddie (Yorkshire)**

BEARDERS' ANSWER: Taking your qualification of 15 overs (presumably six-ball ones giving 90 balls), the fewest runs conceded in an innings in Test cricket are five by R.G. ('Bapu') Nadkarni for India v England at the Corporation Ground in Madras in January 1964. His full analysis was 32-27-5-0. The next most frugal analyses both involved the concession of seven runs in matches against South Africa – by H.L. Collins for Australia at the Old Wanderers, Johannesburg in November 1921 (15-12-7-0), and by Jim Laker for England v South Africa at Cape Town in January 1957 (14.1-9-7-2).

Q Can you please explain to me the circumstances that led to Andy Flower bowling a single ball so far in his Test career? Who was keeping wicket and why only one ball? **Kester Ford, UK**

BEARDERS' ANSWER: It was at Lahore's Gaddafi Stadium on 21 December 1993 during the final day of a 'dead' match. Pakistan had won the first two Tests and this final one had lost 120 overs to seasonal fog and mist.

Zimbabwe dismissed Pakistan for 147 and replied with 230. On that fifth day, after another delayed start, Pakistan took their overnight score of 37-0 to 174-1, Shoaib Mohammad crawling to 53 not out in 325 minutes, before the dismal contest was abandoned as a draw.

In its dying stages, Guy Whittall was unable to bowl the final ball of his 11th over. Andy Flower, Zimbabwe's captain for that series and who describes his mode of delivery as 'right-arm swing', completed that over, probably with his pads on and with Alistair Campbell behind the stumps.

Q I heard that in a recent Test match between West Indies and Sri Lanka, three bowlers were used to complete a single over. Is this a first or has there been any other recorded instance of this in First-Class cricket? **Steve Wedlock, England**

BEARDERS' ANSWER: I am not aware of any recorded similar instance in First-Class cricket, but it may well have happened in a host of matches stretching back nearly 200 years. This was the first instance in Test cricket. It happened at Kandy's Asgiriya Stadium on 21 November 2001 when Mervyn Dillon contracted abdominal pains and was replaced by Colin Stuart after two balls of his third over.

Stuart was banned from bowling for the remainder of the innings by umpire John Hampshire after delivering two high, fast full-tosses (called as no-balls) in his first three balls. Chris Gayle completed the last three balls of the over with his off-breaks.

 In bowling, when was the first recorded use of an overarm delivery? **Mark Peaslee, USA**

BEARDERS' ANSWER: Overarm bowling developed from the round-arm method with which Thomas Walker of Hambledon first experimented in the 1780s.

By 1835, when a revision of the Laws permitted bowlers to raise their hand level with their shoulder (as opposed to elbow), overarm bowling, though illegal, was frequently employed in matches when the umpires turned a blind eye.

The answer to your question is probably 26 August 1862 at the Oval when Edgar Willsher of Kent became the first to be no-balled for bowling overarm. Playing for England against Surrey he was called six times by John Lillywhite for delivering the ball with his hand above his shoulder.

He left the field, his team followed him and play was abandoned for the rest of the day. When Lillywhite refused to accept the legality of Willsher's action, he was replaced as umpire and the reprieved bowler took 6 for 49.

Before Hoggard and Flintoff, when was the last time a Lancastrian and a Yorkshireman opened the bowling in Tests for England? **Mike Shaw, UK**

BEARDERS' ANSWER: When I first saw your brilliant question, Mike, I thought the answer could well be Fred Trueman and Brian Statham in the early 1960s. Then I remembered Peter Martin and Darren Gough but, although they appeared together in three Tests v West Indies in 1995, they did not jointly open the bowling.

Gough and Phil DeFreitas – no, Gough made his debut in 1994, a year after 'Daffy' left Lancashire. Nor did the latter appear in his Red Rose days with Paul Jarvis. Ryan Sidebottom and Paul Allott appeared together once but the latter bowled first change. Allott and Chris Old? No.

Then I found it – in 1971, when Richard Hutton and Peter Lever opened the bowling in both innings against Pakistan at Headingley – the only occasions in his five-Test career that Hutton was given the new ball.

Vintage Years

Q In a pub in Twickenham in 1999, a local was arguing that a bloke called Denis Compton was a better player than Bradman. Can you compare their Test records for me because I thought Denis just sold hair-cream products. **Paul, Australia**

BEARDERS' ANSWER: Must have been a poor night if you can still remember what was said a dozen years ago! Certainly the claimant's judgement must have been slightly influenced by the falling-over water. Denis Compton, one of the first to put his name (and head) to advertising, was one of England's finest batsmen.

A natural games player with a glorious sense of fun, he was one of the greatest improvisers the game has seen. Still England's youngest century-maker, he holds the records for the fastest triple century (181 minutes) and most runs (3,816) and hundreds (18) in a season.

The Don was an absolute genius and about twice as good as the next best batsman in history – something no other sportsman could claim.

Tests: Bradman 52 v Compton 78

Innings: 80 v 131

Not Outs: 10 v 15

Runs: 6,996 v 5,807

Average: 99.94 v 50.06
100s: 29 v 17
50s:13 v 28

(Q) My father used to say that Sir Donald Bradman never did any good in Tests in Lancashire. How many tests did Sir Donald play at Old Trafford and what was his average? **Mal Walker, Australia**

BEARDERS' ANSWER: The Don played three Tests at Old Trafford scoring 81 runs at 27.00 – his innings being 14 (1930), 30 (1934), 7 and 30* (1948). He told me that the light was always so bad there that he couldn't see the ball. Had he been born in Lancashire he might never have played international cricket!

(Q) Ten wickets for 0 runs would be the ultimate bowling performance of course. How close has anyone ever come to that in (a) Test and (b) First-Class cricket? Is Jim Laker's 19 for 90 in 1956 v Australia still up there in terms of the ultimate two-innings performance? **Alastair Munro, Grand Cayman**

BEARDERS' ANSWER: There have been just two 10-wicket innings analyses in Test cricket, Laker's 10 for 53 at Old Trafford, which you mention, and Anil Kumble's

10 for 74 for India v Pakistan at Delhi in 1998–1999.

The cheapest 10-wicket haul in First-Class cricket is Hedley Verity's 10 for 10 for Yorkshire v Nottinghamshire at Headingley in 1932.

I know of one instance in minor cricket of a bowler taking all ten wickets, all bowled, for no runs. This astonishing feat was achieved in just five overs by Jennings Tune on 6 May 1922 in a home Howden and District League match for Cliffe (in Yorkshire) against Eastrington.

No bowler has equalled Laker's 19-wicket match return in either Test or First-Class cricket, but there have been instances of 20-wicket match hauls, all bowled, in minor cricket.

Q Some prose I learnt as a youngster included: 'England 1930 and the seed burst into flower, all of Jackson's grace failed him, Bradman was the power...' Who was 'Jackson'? What's his record? And was he truly graceful? **Paul, Australia**

BEARDERS' ANSWER: F.S. 'Jacker' Jackson epitomised cricket's Golden Age of the Edwardian era. Tall and impressive, he was a stylish middle-order batsman who combined natural timing with a keen appetite for driving and cutting. He bowled right-arm brisk-medium off-cutters with subtle changes of pace and was an athletic fielder in the covers. He captained

Harrow (where the young Winston Churchill was his fag), Cambridge University and England but not his native Yorkshire. He was an inspired leader who skippered England to a 2-0 Ashes victory in 1905 (his final series). He scored 1,415 runs, avge 48.79 with 5 hundreds, in 20 Tests and took 24 wickets, avge 33.29. The Rt Hon Sir Francis Stanley Jackson, GCSI, GCIE, fought in the Boer War, was MP for the Howdenshire division of Yorkshire (1915–1926), financial secretary to the War Office and chairman of the Unionist Party. He narrowly escaped assassination while serving as Governor of Bengal.

Q I have been listening to E.W. Swanton's *Golden Age Of Cricket*, and the phrase 'lob bowler' was used. Can you tell me what a lob bowler is and is there a modern-day lob bowler? **Mike Kimber, Ireland**

BEARDERS' ANSWER: A lob is a slow ball, bowled underarm, usually with a flighted trajectory that made it difficult for the batsman to time without hitting it into the air. Underarm bowling declined rapidly after the legalisation of overarm bowling in 1864 and had virtually disappeared by 1914. The last of its successful exponents were Walter Humphreys (Sussex) who took 148 wickets in 1893 and George Simpson-Hayward who took 23 wickets at 18.26 for England in five Tests against South Africa in 1909–1910, bowling brisk off-breaks along a low trajectory that gripped their matting pitches. The last specialist 'lobster' to appear in county cricket was Trevor James Moloney (1897–1962), who took four wickets in three matches for Surrey in 1921.

Q Apart from Trevor Chappell's underarm ball, who bowled the most recent underarm delivery in Test, First-Class or one-day international cricket? I figure it would have to go back to around 100 years ago. **Daryl Davey, Australia**

BEARDERS' ANSWER: It has certainly happened in English county cricket since the Hitler War. I recall reading reports of Wilf Wooller (Glamorgan) and Charles Palmer (Leicestershire) both resorting to lobs when captaining their counties in the 1950s.

Q Who has hit the most centuries before lunch in Test cricket? Has anyone ever hit a century in each of the three sessions of a day of Test cricket? **westcotoby**

BEARDERS' ANSWER: Four batsmen have scored a hundred before lunch on the first day of a Test. Fourteen others have either added 100 runs to an overnight score or scored a fresh century on other days – Brian Lara is unique in having twice scored/added a pre-lunch century.

Sir Donald Bradman came closest to scoring a hundred in each session when he made 309 runs for Australia against England on the first day at Leeds in 1930 – 105 before lunch, 115 between lunch and tea, and 89 in the final session.

Q Charles Marriott's bowling average in his one Test was 8.72. Is this the best Test bowling average for a bowler who has taken more then 10 wickets? **Captainschoice**

BEARDERS' ANSWER: Yes, it is. The only other bowlers to have taken ten or more wickets at an average under 12.60 also represented England. Kent's Fred ('Nutty') Martin (14 wickets for 141 runs in two Tests) was a left-arm bowler very similar in pace and style to Derek Underwood. Surrey's George Lohmann (112 wickets for 1,205 runs in 18 Tests) was a brisk-medium right-hander who has the strongest statistical claim to be considered the greatest Test-match bowler of all time.

Q Please inform me as to who is the youngest and who is the oldest batsman to score 100 runs for England in a Test. **Ronald Nuttall, England**

BEARDERS' ANSWER: Hi Nutters (Blackpool's scorer and an invaluable checker of the individual bests in *Playfair Cricket Annual*). Thanks for a nice easy one!

Denis Compton is the youngest and Jack Hobbs the oldest to score a Test match century for England. 'Compo' was 20 years 19 days old when he completed his 102 against the 1938 Australians at Trent Bridge. It was his first Test against Australia, and his partnership of 206 in 138 minutes with Eddie Paynter remains the England record in Ashes Tests.

'The Master' had lived 46 years and 82 days when he made 142 at Melbourne in March 1929, and that remains the record age for any batsman scoring a Test hundred. It was his 15th Test hundred and his 12th against Australia (still the England record).

The subject matter is Martha Grace. I have for some time been researching into this most interesting of women, yet there is very little known of her. I have visited Glynis Williams at Lord's and also Hugh Chevallier at Wisden. The British Library have nothing, although her father George Pocock was better known for his kite-flying activities! Any ideas from you would be appreciated. **Terry Rogers, England**

BEARDERS' ANSWER: Simon Rae's excellent biography *W.G. Grace – A Life*, published in 1998 by Faber and Faber, includes details of many aspects of the life of the

Champion's mother. They include her marriage, family, life both in Downend and at The Chestnuts, and her interest in cricket. Martha Grace appears on 22 of this work's 548 pages. George Pocock did indeed allow his daughter 'the daring honour' of becoming 'the first Aeropleust' and launched W.G. Grace's mother-to-be into the sky, strapped into his kite-carriage – a chair attached to an array of huge kites.

Q Looking at the line-up of the last England team [before the 2006–2007 Ashes] to be whitewashed in Australia, I noticed that Bert Strudwick was a number 11 wicket-keeper. With the exception of Tom Campbell of South Africa, have there been any other number 11 wicket-keepers in Test cricket? **Rupert (Barnes, London)**

BEARDERS' ANSWER: As a bowler, captain or selector who would always pick the most reliable gloveman and leave the specialist batsman to accept their responsibility for scoring runs, I was sufficiently intrigued by your question, Rupert, to devote several hours to combing the scores of 1,888 international Test matches to compile a detailed survey – and by a distance the longest answer I have given to any question in this series.

Although virtually unheard of in modern times, it was not an uncommon policy in the Victorian era, particularly with regard to England teams. Joe Hunter

(Yorkshire), against Australia at Adelaide in 1884–1885 (the 17th Test match), was the first wicket-keeper to bat at number 11 in Test cricket. His international career was confined to that five-match series and he batted last in each of his seven innings.

A search of those early scores reveals that Richard Pilling (Lancashire) batted last in the final four of his 13 Test innings (1886–1888); Mordecai Sherwin (Nottinghamshire), at just under 17 stone probably the heaviest Test wicket-keeper of all time, batted last in each of his six innings in 1886–1887 and 1888; Harry Wood (Surrey) batted next to the roller in the first of his four innings, also in 1888; and Harry Butt (Sussex) was at 11 for three of his four innings in South Africa in 1895–1896. In the same period, two Australian keepers went in last: Fred Burton (twice in 1886–1887) and Jack Blackham (11 times between 1891–1892 and 1893).

From the turn of the century until the 1914–1918 war, seven wicket-keepers batted last, including three in the 1912 Triangular Tournament: Dick Lilley (England; 1 – 1903–1904); James Kelly (Australia; 4 – 1902–1905); Percy Sherwell (South Africa; 3 – 1905–1906); 'Sammy' Carter (Australia; 4 – 1909 to 1911–1912); Tom Campbell (South Africa; 4 – 1909–1910 to 1912); Tommy Ward (South Africa; 10 – 1912); William Carkeek (Australia; 3 – 1912).

Bert Strudwick, who was Surrey's scorer when I began my *TMS* career, was number 11 in 25 (the record by a distance) of his 42 innings between 1909–1910 and

1926. George Duckworth (Lancashire; 11 – 1928–1929 to 1930–1931), Errol Hunte (West Indies; 2 in 1929–1930), and Ken James (New Zealand; 3 – 1931 and 1931–1932) provided the only other instances between the wars.

Since 1945, eighteen keepers have batted at 11 in Test cricket: Dattaram Hindlekar (India; 3 in 1946); 'Jenni' Irani (India; 3 in 1947–1948); Probir Sen (India; 1 in 1951–1952); Gil Langley (Australia; 6 – 1953 to 1956–1957); Ian Colquhoun (New Zealand; 2 in 1954–1955); Godfrey Evans (England; 2 in 1955 and 1958–1959, the last England keeper to bat that low and only because he had fractured a finger); Trevor McMahon (New Zealand; 3 in 1955–1956); Len Maddocks (Australia; 1 in 1956); Wally Grout (Australia; 5 in 1960–1961 to 1963–1964); Budhi Kunderan (India; 2 in 1961–1962); Barry Jarman (Australia; 3 in 1962–1963); John Ward (New Zealand; 4 in 1964–1965 and 1965); Roy Harford (New Zealand: 5 in 1967–1968); Barry Milburn (New Zealand; 3 in 1968–1969); Wasim Bari (Pakistan; 4 in 1976–1977); Syed Kirmani (India; 2 in 1983–1984); Guy de Alwis (Sri Lanka; 1 in 1986–1987); Nayan Mongia (India; 1 in 1999–2000).

As the last two instances involved keepers being demoted from higher first innings batting positions, it is 25 years (30 October 1983) and 923 matches since a wicket-keeper (Kirmani) batted at number 11 in the first innings of a Test. The last keeper to bat even as low as number 10 in Test cricket was Thami Tsolekile

for South Africa v India at Calcutta in November/
December 2004.

 Who was the first man to score a double
century in one innings at Lord's? **Matt, UK**

BEARDERS' ANSWER: William Ward (1787–1849) – his
278 for MCC v Norfolk in 1820 was also the first
double century in all First-Class cricket. He played for
Surrey (1815–1817) and Hampshire (1816–1845) and
was MP for the City of London from 1826 to 1831.

 Who was the last person to hit a six over the
Lord's pavilion? **Wilmagreen**

BEARDERS' ANSWER: Albert Trott (Victoria, Middlesex,
Australia and England) is the only batsman who has
struck a ball over top of the Lord's pavilion. He achieved
this unique feat on 31 July 1899 off the bowling of
Monty Noble while batting for the MCC and Ground
against the Australians.

 Can you tell me who scored the first century in
Limited-Overs Internationals? **P. Behary, India**

BEARDERS' ANSWER: Dennis Amiss – he scored 103 for England v Australia at Old Trafford in 1972 in the second limited-overs international, the first having been staged at the MCG on 5 January 1971 when the Melbourne Test match was abandoned through rain.

Q As a relative of Frank Woolley, I was wondering whether you could tell me how many people have beaten his 2,000 runs and 100 wickets in a season?
Robin Woolley, England

BEARDERS' ANSWER: Very good to hear from you, Robin. Regrettably I never had the great pleasure of seeing Frank play, but I met him at Canterbury when he was in his mid-seventies. Brian Johnston complimented him on his ramrod straight back. 'Haven't been able to bend it for 20 years,' he replied.

Only two players have surpassed the 2,000 runs/100 wickets double which your ancestor achieved a record four times (1914, 1921, 1922, 1923). Yorkshire's G.H. (George) Hirst uniquely achieved the double 'double' when he scored 2,385 runs and took 208 wickets in 1906. J.H. ('Jim' senior) Parks of Sussex scored 3,003 runs and took 101 wickets in 1937.

Q Two questions, both related to age and prompted by our game against Coaver CC on Sunday. Our 67-year-old opening bat scored a ton on Sunday. He has now scored club cricket centuries in each of six decades, his first being in 1959. Has anyone heard of this being done before? Have any First-Class players managed tons in more than three decades? **Charles Sheldrick (Cheriton Fitzpaine CC)**

BEARDERS' ANSWER: I toured India in 1991–1992 with a remarkable batsman, Jack Hyams, who was then 72 and, having scored hundreds every season since he began playing in his late-teens, had amassed over 60,000 runs. Apparently he still plays occasionally in his late eighties, so I suspect he might have at least equalled your colleague's remarkable feat.

As Jack Hobbs scored his maiden First-Class hundred in 1905 (including 137 before lunch against Essex, the county that had spurned first option on his services) and his last in 1934, his 197 centuries were gathered during four decades. He remains the oldest (46 years 82 days) to score a hundred in Test cricket.

Q The name of my great uncle, A.P. 'Tich' Freeman, is, of course, very well known to serious cricket fans. I believe he had a brother and also some cousins named Russell who played for Essex – what is known about their careers? **Phil Neatherway, England**

BEARDERS' ANSWER: The only bowler to take 300 wickets in a season (304 in 1928), 'Tich' Freeman achieved phenomenally consistent success for Kent with 2,090 of his 3,776 wickets coming in just eight seasons. Selected for only a dozen Tests, the 5ft 2in leg-spinner took 66 wickets at 25.86. After bowling 154,414 balls in First-Class cricket, he named his final home 'Dunbowlin'.

Four of his relatives played First-Class cricket. His brother (J.R.), nephew (E.C.) and cousin (E.J.) all appeared for Essex, while his uncle (D.P.) played for Kent. You will find their details in the *Who's Who of Cricketers*, published by Hamlyn in association with the ACS in 1993. I can find no record of Freeman being related to the Essex Russells.

Q Many, many years ago I read or heard about a fielder who displayed his prowess during an interval with a demonstration whereby he fielded three balls in succession and threw down each stump in turn. Any idea who this was? **Tom, Sweden**

BEARDERS' ANSWER: The fielder was Colin Bland, a Rhodesian-born, right-handed batsman who represented South Africa in 21 Tests. The outstanding ground fielder and thrower of his era, he achieved exceptional accuracy through hours of practice. During an interval when the touring team was playing Kent at Canterbury in 1965, Bland demonstrated his skill for the BBC television cameras. Three stumps were arranged as a wicket in front of netting. Within a minute, he fielded three balls thrown a distance from him, swivelled and threw down the stumps in turn from about 20 yards. It is that black and white TV film which you will have seen.

Q I have recently finished reading a dusty copy of Wally Hammond's *Cricket – My World*. The book is full of anecdotes and tales from back in the day, though one story towards the end was beyond my comprehension. While discussing the workload placed on bowlers at all levels, Wally speaks of his concern about individuals being over-bowled and injured as a result. He then gives the example of a chap referred to only as 'Shaw', who once bowled more than 100 overs in a day – as a result of this he injured his foot and never played again. Now I don't want to accuse Wally of being liberal with the truth, but how is this possible? Does any record exist of this incredible feat of bowling stamina? Unfortunately, no first name or county team/fixture is given. **Roland James**

BEARDERS' ANSWER: Fascinating question, Roland. Hammond was referring to Alfred Shaw, the renowned right-arm, slow-medium bowler who appeared in 404 First-Class matches for Nottinghamshire, Sussex, the MCC and England between 1864 and 1897. His 2,027 wickets included 177 five-wicket innings hauls. On 44 occasions he took ten or more in a match. In an era of four-ball overs, he bowled a grand total of 101,967 balls – the equivalent of almost 17,000 six-ball overs. He sent down over 10,500 balls (1,750 six-ball overs) in 1876 and 1878. However, on only one occasion did he bowl 100 four-ball overs in an innings (100.1 for Sussex v Notts at Trent Bridge in 1895), but they were not all on the same day. Yet he may have sent down 100 overs when the opposition batted twice on the same day.

Q I understand that the number on the England players' shirts relates to the number of players who have ever played Test cricket for England. However, this begs another question – who was (or would have been) number one? My wife suggests Dr W.G. Grace. Is she correct? **Simon Dykins, England**

BEARDERS' ANSWER: I'm afraid she isn't. How much have you won? W.G. did not play in the first three Tests (in Australia in 1876–1877 and 1878–1879). Twenty players had represented England before he made his debut at the Oval in 1880.

Malcolm Ashton, the former BBC TV scorer now with Channel Four and the ECB's scorer on overseas tours, has been commissioned to produce a numbered register of England Test cricketers.

I assume that it is being done alphabetically and that Thomas Armitage, a tall, robust Yorkshire all-rounder who played in the first two Tests, will be given # 1. W.G. will probably be No. 24.

Q What is the biggest partnership ever in First-Class cricket? Someone said it might have been when Lara got 501, but I wasn't sure. Can you help and end the arguing in the pub? **Mark Waugh, UK**

BEARDERS' ANSWER: The highest partnership for any wicket in all First-Class matches is 577 for the fourth wicket between Vijay Hazare (288) and Gul Mahomed (319) for Baroda v Holkar at Baroda, India, in the Final of the Ranji Trophy in March 1947. It took 533 minutes. They came together with the score 39 for 3. Baroda totalled 784 and went on to win the match by an innings and 409 runs.

Q I have a bet that a batsman playing against Kent (for Nottinghamshire?) in a four-day County Championship match scored a double century in each innings but was on the losing side. **John Pepper**

BEARDERS' ANSWER: You lose your bet, John! Only one batsman in the entire history of First-Class cricket has scored double centuries in both innings of a match. Playing for Kent against Essex at Castle Park, Colchester, in 1938, Arthur Fagg contributed 244 and 202 not out to a drawn contest.

Q Many years ago, I was told that Sir Don Bradman once scored an incredible 100 off one over with many no-balls in a club/school/non-First-Class game. Can this possibly be true? **Richard Webber, England**

BEARDERS' ANSWER: There were no no-balls involved. The Don scored 100 runs off 22 balls in three eight-ball overs during his innings at Blackheath, NSW, a Blue Mountains town some 60 miles west of Sydney, on 3 November 1931.

Playing for Blackheath against Lithgow in a match to celebrate the opening of an experimental malthoid pitch, Bradman, having scored 38 off the first over he received, later in his innings produced the following record-breaking sequence: 66424461/64466464/*661*446. (* denote singles scored by his partner, Wendell Bill).

Q I have **The Don Declares**, a series of ABC interviews with Bradman made in 1988. In one tape, he recounts how, on one tour, he just managed to score 1,000 runs in May on the last possible day. I suspect that with changed schedules this is now an impossible event for a county player. However, I can't find any details of this odd record. How often was it done? How often by a tourist? Who did it in the fewest innings? **Bill Cashin, Aust/UK**

BEARDERS' ANSWER: The Don did NOT score 1,000 First-Class runs IN MAY. Only three players have achieved that feat: W.G. Grace (Gloucestershire) in 1895, W.R. Hammond (Gloucestershire) in 1927, and C. Hallows (Lancashire) in 1928.

Bradman, in company with T.W. Hayward (Surrey, 1900), W.J. Edrich (Middlesex, 1938), G.M. Turner (New Zealanders, 1973) and G.A. Hick (Worcestershire, 1988) scored 1,000 First-Class runs BEFORE JUNE (i.e. in April and May). He is alone in doing so twice (1930 and 1938).

As that list shows, Glenn Turner is the only other touring player to achieve this. The Don holds the record for the fewest innings in the second category, with seven in 1938. W.G. needed fewest innings (10) to reach 1,000 runs in May alone.

 Who captained England at cricket and played rugby for Wales? **Andrew, England**

BEARDERS' ANSWER: No one!
Maurice Turnbull played in nine Tests for England

(1929–1930 to 1936), captained Cambridge University in his final year and Glamorgan for 10 seasons, and gained two rugby union caps for Wales in 1932–1933. He also represented Wales at hockey and was squash champion for South Wales. He is the only one to play cricket for England and rugby for Wales but he did not captain England. As a major in the Welsh Guards, he was killed instantly by a sniper's bullet during the Normandy landings in 1944.

A.R. (Tony) Lewis is the only Welshman to captain England at cricket. He gained a blue for rugby at Cambridge but a knee injury effectively ended his football career.

 . Has England ever played an official Test in the United States? **John, US**

BEARDERS' ANSWER: The USA has never staged an official Test, although, in 1844, New York was the venue of cricket's first international match (against Canada).

The first touring team actually to reach its objective overseas was the English expedition to Canada and America in 1859. Organised by Fred Lillywhite, it was captained by George Parr and included John Wisden.

Philadelphia staged First-Class matches between 1878 and 1913 and toured Britain in 1884, 1889, 1897, 1903 and 1908. Their greatest player was John Barton King (1873–1965), a right-arm, fast swing bowler who headed the English averages in 1908 with 87 wickets at 11.01 and subsequently took all ten wickets in a First-Class match.

May I recommend to you 'A Guide to First Class and Other Important Cricket Matches in North and South America' by C.J. Clynes, published by the Association of Cricket Statisticians (3 Radcliffe Road, West Bridgford, Nottingham NG2 5FF).

Ⓠ What is the longest run of games by a major side without a win against Test-playing nations?
Andrew, UK

BEARDERS' ANSWER: New Zealand holds that unfortunate record. After their inaugural Test in January 1930, they played 44 Tests before gaining their first victory 26 years later, against West Indies at Auckland on 13 March 1956. Curiously, that initial victory was completed with a stumping by Simpson Guillen, a Trinidadian who was making the last of his three appearances for New Zealand after gaining five caps for West Indies.

The County Game

Has there been any instance when a captain has won the man-of-match award purely for captaincy in the field? **Richay Vora, USA**

BEARDERS' ANSWER: I can think of only one, Richay. John Abrahams was given the Gold Award by Peter May when Lancashire beat Warwickshire by six wickets to win the 1984 Benson and Hedges Cup final.

Apart from winning the toss and holding a catch at mid-wicket, he made little impact on the match, being caught at the wicket third ball. It was his 32nd birthday though!

What is the highest number of First-Class wickets taken by a non-Test player? **Rob, England**

BEARDERS' ANSWER: Fascinating question, Rob. The answer is 2,218 at 22.32 by Don Shepherd, the first bowler to take 2,000 wickets for Glamorgan. His tally from a career spanning 23 summers (1950–1972) included 100 wickets in a season 12 times, 28 instances of ten or more in a match and 123 of five or more in an innings.

His best was 9 for 47. A hard-hitting lower-order batsman, he hit 51 against the 1961 Australians with just 11 scoring strokes: six sixes, three fours, a two and a single.

 What's the most number of First-Class runs scored in a season, and by whom? **Nick Dymoke-Marr, UK**

BEARDERS' ANSWER: Denis Compton holds that record with 3,816 runs, average 90.85, including a record 18 hundreds, in 1947. No one is likely to approach this aggregate because the intrusion of limited-overs cricket has greatly decreased the number of First-Class innings a batsman can play. Last season [2005] the highest number was 33 innings, 17 fewer than Compton enjoyed. No one has scored 3,000 runs in a season since 1961 when Bill Alley (Somerset) made 3,019 from 64 innings.

I was at the old Hampshire ground at Northlands Road in 1996 when Kevan James took four wickets in four balls and then followed it up with a century in the same match against India. Vic Isaacs (Hampshire scorer) said at the time that this was unprecedented. Has anyone else achieved this all-round feat in First-Class cricket, or has anyone come close? **Paul Little, England**

BEARDERS' ANSWER: Vic is absolutely correct, and the feat of Kevan James remains unique. Nine players have scored a century and taken a hat-trick in the same First-Class match, M.J. ('Mike') Procter doing so twice. One of them, W.E. (William) Roller, scored 204 and took a hat-trick for Surrey.

Q I have a cricket stump, split in two and hinged. When opened, the signatures of both teams, Kent XI & Essex, are on each half of the stump. Is it possible to find out when the match was played and if the stump is worth anything to a collector?

The teams are: Essex – Trevor Bailey, R. Horsefield, Doug Insole, R. Preston, W. Greensmith, F.C. Down, T. Rist, Reg Smith, A. Avery, Peter Smith and A.N. Other; Kent – S. Wright, B.E. Edrich, A.S. Fagg, Ray Wovey, Peter Hearn, M. Shant (?), S. Leary, R. Mays, S. Kimms, W. Turreywood, H. Lucas. Thanks for trying. **Mick Green, England**

BEARDERS' ANSWER: Certainly the most intriguing puzzle I have been set for some while – especially when some of the names were illegible! 'S. Kimms' (alias S.E.A.

Kimmins) provides the vital clue, because he appeared for Kent only in 1950 and 1951. Essex and Kent played each other home and away in both those seasons and the nearest matching to the names on your stump is with the team who played at Ilford on 2–5 June 1951.

In your order they were: ESSEX – T.E. Bailey, R. Horsfall, D.J. Insole, K.C. Preston, W.T. Greensmith, T.C. Dodds, P.A. Gibb, R. (Ray) Smith, A.V. Avery, T.P.B. (Peter) Smith, C. Griffiths; KENT – D.V.P. Wright, B.R. Edrich, A.E. Fagg, R.R. Dovey, P. Hearn, T.G. Evans, S.E. Leary, R. Mayes, S.E.A. Kimmins, W. Murray-Wood, A.H. Phebey.

Your list includes a Rist (F.H.?) and a Lucas (F.C.?) who may have been the 12th Men. 'M. Shant' must be either Evans or Phebey. Value – depends on your finding the right collector. Probably at least £100 because it is over 50 years old and most of the signatories have been claimed by the Great Scorer.

Q Has there ever been a case where all 11 members of the fielding side have been directly involved in dismissing the batting side, and had their names on the scorecard? **Peter, Canada**

BEARDERS' ANSWER: I have found only one instance in First-Class matches, Peter, and I probably would not have noticed it if I had not been scoring the match for a BBC commentary. It occurred at Grace Road,

Leicester, in August 1967 when Northamptonshire were dismissed for 211 in reply to their host's 340.

All ten wickets fell to catches by ten different fielders. Jack Birkenshaw was the only one not to take a catch, and he took three wickets. Leicestershire declared their second innings at 147 for 6 and dismissed Northants for 113 to win by 163 runs. Their captain, Tony Lock, took 7 for 75 and 6 for 43.

Q Has any wicket-keeper ever stumped four batsmen off four consecutive balls as I did during a Sunday league game for Whittington CC (Staffordshire)?
Ian Duffell

BEARDERS' ANSWER: My records of minor cricket do not extend as far as most stumpings off consecutive balls. Such is the long history and vast volume of cricket at that level worldwide that I expect it has happened before and, hopefully, someone will email me with the details!

The closest instance in First-Class cricket was achieved by William Henry Brain when he performed a hat-trick of stumpings off C.L. (Charlie) Townsend, a 16-year-old Clifton schoolboy playing for Gloucestershire v Somerset at Cheltenham while on holiday in 1893.

Q I remember one of the commentators asking you to find out which county had produced the most England Test captains. Sadly I was on my way to the airport at the time and missed your answer! **Boredkentjames**

BEARDERS' ANSWER: Kevin Pietersen is England's 78th Test captain. Middlesex has provided the most with 12: G.O.B. Allen, J.M. Brearley, J.E. Emburey, M.W. Gatting, F.G. Mann, F.T. Mann, T.C. O'Brien, R.W.V. Robins, G.T.S. Stevens, A.E. Stoddart, P.F. Warner and A.J. Strauss. Distribution for the other 17 counties is: eight – Surrey, Yorkshire; seven – Lancashire, Sussex; six – Kent ; five – Essex, four – Nottinghamshire, Warwickshire; three – Hampshire, Somerset, Worcestershire; two – Gloucestershire, Leicestershire, Northamptonshire; one – Derbyshire, Glamorgan; none – Durham.

Q I seem to remember that in the distant past the Warwickshire spinner Eric Hollies once took all ten wickets in a county match unassisted. Is my memory playing tricks? **Swanwestx**

BEARDERS' ANSWER: Eric Hollies did indeed take all ten (for 49 runs off 20.4 overs) against Nottinghamshire at Edgbaston on 24 July 1946 without the aid of fielders. He bowled seven of his victims and trapped the other three leg before. His feat could not prevent Nottinghamshire from gaining an eight-wicket victory in two days. Two years later, Hollies bowled Don Bradman second ball in his final Test match innings to reduce the great man's career batting average to fractionally below 100.

Q On 14 August 1958, in arguably one of the most astonishing days in First-Class cricket history, the second day of the match between Derbyshire and Hampshire at Burton upon Trent, no fewer than 39 wickets fell. Derbyshire, resuming at 8-1 in its first innings, were dismissed for 74, before skittling Hampshire for 23. The hosts reached 107 second time round, while the visitors managed only 55. Is this the record number of wickets in a single day in a First-Class match? **Bob Letham (Bridgend, Wales)**

BEARDERS' ANSWER: That instance equalled the record of 39 wickets set on 28 May 1880 when Oxford University (53 and 75) lost to the MCC (89 and 41 for 9) by one wicket in a single day.

Q A friend recently told me about her grandfather, Edward Mathieson, who apparently played county cricket. Do you have any information on him? **C.K. Mullins, Scotland**

BEARDERS' ANSWER: No one has appeared in county cricket under the name of Mathieson. The nearest I can find is Edward Matheson who was born at Charlton in London on 14 June 1865 and died in Devon at Uffculme, near Tiverton, on 26 February 1945. He was educated at the Clergy Orphan School in Canterbury.

A right-handed, middle-order batsman, he made his First-Class debut for the South of England v the Australians at Hastings in 1886, scoring 1 and 6. He had to wait 13 seasons before undertaking the second half of his career, appearing for Warwickshire v Gloucestershire at Bristol and scoring 9 and, opening, 5. The product of this two-match career was 21 runs, average 5.25, and a catch. He was not invited to bowl.

Having read this, your friend will almost certainly deny any relationship to this cricketer!

Q A couple of years ago, one county had three sets of brothers and the father to one of these pair of brothers on their books. Which county was it, and had any other county done it before? **Barry Dyke, UK**

BEARDERS' ANSWER: In 1999, Surrey's staff included the brothers Bicknell (Darren and Martin), Butcher (Gary and Mark) and Hollioake (Adam and Ben). The Butchers' father, Alan, was the 2nd XI Coach and had played a County Championship match in an emergency the previous season.

In 1938, three sets of brothers represented Sussex in the County Championship: James and John Langridge, Charlie and John Oakes, and Harry and Jim (sr) Parks. A brace of unrelated Cornfords (Jim and Walter) also featured. No fewer than seven Foster brethren represented Worcestershire during the period 1899–1934, with six appearing during the seasons 1908–1911. The full list, with Worcestershire careers in brackets is: B.S. (1902–1911), G.N. (1903–1914), H.K. (1899–1925), M.K. (1908–1934), N.J.A. (1914–1923), R.E. (1899–1912) and W.L. (1899–1911). Not surprisingly the county became known as 'Fostershire'.

Q Who was the first non-Yorkshire-born player to play First-Class cricket for Yorkshire? **Patrick Jones, Wales**

BEARDERS' ANSWER: If we accept the First Class List of Matches compiled by the ACS (Association of Cricket Statisticians and Historians), then Thomas Rawson Barker, born at Bakewell, Derbyshire, was the first.

A right-handed batsman and left round-arm, medium-pace bowler, he appeared in Yorkshire's inaugural First-Class match at the Hyde Park Ground in Sheffield in 1833 against Norfolk. A lead merchant in Sheffield, he served as mayor and, when the Yorkshire County Cricket Club was formed in 1863, he became its first President.

In a Championship match against Warwickshire, D.M. Benkenstein scored 167 not out for Durham but ended up on the losing side. There are probably many tail-enders who have managed a similar 'not out' feat, but who claims the distinction of the highest total not out figure for a losing side in a First-Class game? **Alan Nicholson, England**

BEARDERS' ANSWER: Percy Perrin scored a career-best 343 not out for Essex (597 and 97) against Derbyshire (548 and 149-1) at Chesterfield in 1904, the hosts winning an extraordinary match by nine wickets. In a lengthy First-Class career (1896 to 1928 inclusive), he amassed 29,709 runs, average 35.92, with 66 hundreds, but was never picked for England. However, Perrin did become a Test Selector (1926 and 1931–1939), and was Chairman in the final pre-war season.

Who has scored the most First-Class runs and never played Test cricket? Also, who has taken the most wickets and never played a Test? **Aaron (Newcastle-upon-Tyne)**

BEARDERS' ANSWER: Both those unfortunate records go to Welsh-born Glamorgan players. Alan Jones (born in Velindre), amassed the 35th highest First-Class runs aggregate: 36,049 runs, average 32.89 with 56 hundreds. The only player to gain an England cap in the 1970 Rest of the World series and not play in any official Tests, he was asked by the TCCB to return it, with his blazer, when the ICC removed Test status from those five matches several years later. Curiously, both items had mysteriously disappeared.

Don Shepherd (Port Eynon) is 22nd on the First-Class wickets tally with 2,218 wickets at 21.32 runs apiece. An outstanding bowler of off-spin and cutters, he has been a stalwart of Radio Wales commentaries since he retired in 1972.

Q As a hardy Gloucestershire CCC supporter, I was wondering whether you knew the last time – excluding Surrey this year – when a county side went a whole season without a Championship victory. If it goes back to the 1890s, I don't want to know! **Mark Kingston (Wiltshire)**

BEARDERS' ANSWER: You only have to backtrack to 1996, Mark. It should provide Gloucestershire with a tad of hope to find that the county who suffered that ignominy was this year's Division I champions, Durham. However, Gloucestershire are the first Division II team to fail to win a single match since the two-division system was introduced in 2000. They have relieved Derbyshire (2001, 2004 and 2005), Durham (2002) and Glamorgan (2007) of the record for the fewest Division II victories in a season, namely one!

Which English county holds the record for having the largest number of players in the England team at one time, and when did this happen? **William, Yorkshire**

BEARDERS' ANSWER: Nottinghamshire with 6 (W. Barnes, W. Flowers, W. Gunn, W.H. Scotton, M. Sherwin and A. Shrewsbury) v Australia at Sydney in January 1887.

 Two years ago in a 48-over league match for my club, we recorded victory by 375 runs. We batted first and made 399 then bowled the opposition out for 24. Are there any circumstances in professional limited-overs cricket where a team has recorded a victory of this size? **Chinny, Cornwall**

BEARDERS' ANSWER: My records of domestic limited-overs cricket are not exhaustive beyond the international and UK arenas. The closest I can find is the 346-run margin by which Somerset beat Devon at Torquay in the 1990 NatWest Trophy. The record runs margin at international level is a mere 245.

 Has any batsman ever scored a double century in each innings of any First-Class match? **Shamoon, India**

BEARDERS' ANSWER: Just one. Arthur Fagg, who played in five Tests (1936–1939) and subsequently umpired in another 18, scored 244 and 202 not out for Kent v Essex at Colchester in 1938.

His match aggregate of 446 remained the First-Class record in England until 1990 when Graham Gooch scored 333 and 123 for England against India at Lord's.

 How many times has the same county won both the County Championship and the Second XI Championship in the same season? **Ray Grace (Haltwhistle)**

BEARDERS' ANSWER: Since the Second XI Championship was inaugurated in 1959, four counties have won both titles: Kent (1970), Middlesex (1993), Sussex (2007) and Durham (2008).

Who was the first County batsman to be given out having handled the ball? **Satish Salve, India**

BEARDERS' ANSWER: That honour goes to George ('Farmer') Bennett of Kent. Playing against Sussex at Hove in August 1872, he had not got off the mark when he removed a ball that had lodged in his clothing.

This was before the introduction of Law 33 (b) in 1899, which declared such a ball to be 'dead'.

 Which was the first county to score 800 runs in an innings? **Joan Cowlard, England**

BEARDERS' ANSWER: Lancashire were the first to reach that mark when they scored 801 in just eight hours against Somerset at Taunton on 15–16 July 1895. A.C. (Archie) MacLaren scored the then record First-Class score of 424, overtaking W.G. Grace's 344 that had stood since 1876. The following season Yorkshire scored 887 against Warwickshire at Edgbaston.

 In July 1975, I saw Colin Cowdrey make an unbeaten century for Kent v Gloucestershire at Cheltenham. I am curious to know if this was Cowdrey's last First-Class century, as I know he pretty much retired at the end of 1975. **Chris Simpson, Abidjan, Ivory Coast**

BEARDERS' ANSWER: Chris, thank you for adding to the continuing spread of exotic locations of our questioners. Yes, you did see Colin Cowdrey score the last of his 107 First-Class hundreds when he scored that 119 not out. A month earlier he had hit an undefeated hundred for

Kent against the Australians, but the tourists exacted their revenge when Dennis Lillee dismissed him for a pair when he captained the MCC at Lord's the following week.

Recalled from retirement for a solitary appearance in 1976, he scored 25 and 15 against Surrey in the Canterbury Week.

Q Please remind me, in which one-day final did Sir Geoffrey score 146 for Yorkshire? **Geoff, Yorkshire**

BEARDERS' ANSWER: Geoffrey Boycott scored 146 for Yorkshire v Surrey in the 1965 Gillette Cup Final. It remains the highest score in a Lord's county limited-overs final.

Q Who has scored three consecutive centuries at Lord's? **Jhansi, India**

BEARDERS' ANSWER: It has not been achieved in Test matches but, captaining Middlesex in 1995, Mike Gatting scored 101 v Sussex, 148 v Nottinghamshire and 136 v Kent in successive First-Class innings at Lord's.

I'm told that my distant relative Alf Gover was so successful because as Surrey senior professional he bowled only to batsmen he knew he could easily dismiss. Is there anything in his record to support this allegation? **John, UK**

I had the pleasure of knowing Alf Gover well (we were born in the same Epsom hospital) and would dismiss any such allegation as arrant nonsense. He certainly would not have got away with it under the Surrey captaincies of Percy Fender, Douglas Jardine or Errol Holmes. His record of taking 100 wickets in a season eight times would suggest that he knew a lot of batsmen he could dismiss, notably in 1936 and 1937 when he took 200 wickets. He remains the only fast bowler to reach that milestone since his Surrey predecessor Tom Richardson in 1897.

 What is the highest partnership between batsmen numbers 10 and 11? **Ed, England**

BEARDERS' ANSWER: The record in all First-Class cricket is 249 in 190 minutes by C.T. (Chandra) Sarwate (124 not out) and S.N. (Shute) Banerjee (121) for the 1946 Indians against Surrey at the Oval. Joining forces at 205 for 9, they took the total to 454. Bowled out for 135, Surrey followed on and made 338, Sarwate's leg-breaks claiming five victims, and lost by nine wickets. Banerjee was the first Bengali to play international cricket.

The Test match record, also created at the Oval, is 128 in 140 minutes by Ken Higgs (63) and John Snow (59 not out) for England v West Indies in 1966, both batsmen registering their maiden First-Class fifties.

Well, Fancy That!

How many England captains were not born in England? **Simon Wenham, UK**

BEARDERS' ANSWER: I can offer 14 of the 73: Lord Harris (Trinidad), T.C. O'Brien (Ireland), P.F. Warner (Trinidad), D.R. Jardine (India), G.O.B. Allen (Australia), F.R. Brown (Peru), D.B. Carr (Germany), M.C. Cowdrey (India), E.R. Dexter (Italy), A.R. Lewis (Wales), M.H. Denness (Scotland), A.W. Greig (South Africa), A.J. Lamb (South Africa), N. Hussain (India).

Why do the badges on the England shirts sometimes appear on the opposite sleeves? Someone suggested it depends on the way that the wearer bats. **Mark Osborn, England**

BEARDERS' ANSWER: That 'someone' is absolutely right. Right-handed batsmen's shirts have their main logos on the left sleeve and left-handers on their right ones so that they face the camera from the bowler's end when they are taking strike.

(Q) Why do some batsmen have white tape on the underside of the peak on their helmets? Is this to improve the amount of light reaching their eyes? **David Milne, UK**

BEARDERS' ANSWER: Three possible reasons:

1. To reflect the light from near their eyes as you suggest.

2. Because the peak is damaged from being either struck by balls or crammed into their cricket case.

3. A convenient place to store tape for repairing injuries to themselves or their bat.

(Q) As I recall, the career of former Aussie Test batsman Ian Redpath was ended by an injury caused when he over-exuberantly appealed for a wicket off his own bowling during a World Series Cricket match. Is this factual? **Joe Ezekiel, USA**

BEARDERS' ANSWER: Yes, it is, Joe. He severely damaged his undercarriage when he leapt in the air celebrating a rare victim of his occasional bowling.

He returned to his antique business and became

an active politician. 'Redders' continued to play the occasional social and charity match and appeared for an Old Australia XI against Sir Paul Getty's Old England XI at Wormsley as recently as July 2001.

(Q) Which member of the 1966 England World Cup-winning squad also played County cricket and which County did he represent? **Roddy Porter, United Kingdom**

BEARDERS' ANSWER: That was Geoffrey Charles Hurst, who scored a hat-trick of goals in that World Cup final. A useful wicket-keeper and right-handed lower-order batsman, he was also an outstanding fielder.

It was that last attribute which prompted Trevor Bailey, then captain of Essex, to select him for a solitary First-Class appearance against Lancashire at Liverpool in 1962. He contributed two catches but no runs (0* and 0) to an Essex victory.

(Q) In this summer's [2008] Twenty20 match between England and New Zealand, Ravi Bopara was making his debut in this form of the game and neither batted nor bowled. Have there been any other players that have had a similarly inactive international career, in any form of the game? I recall mention of a poor chap some years ago who was called up for his debut Test, only for rain to intervene. **William**

BEARDERS' ANSWER: Bopara has hardly had an 'inactive international career'. Prior to the limited-overs phase of South Africa's current tour, he has played in three Tests and 26 fifty-overs internationals. He is likely to play in their imminent 20-overs game at Chester-le-Street.

John Crawford William ('Jack') MacBryan, a stylish Somerset and Cambridge University batsman, was the cricketer you mention. Selected for the Fourth Test against South Africa in 1924 in a contest involving just 165 minutes of play, his Test career fell victim to Manchester's notorious climate, and he remains the only Test cricketer who did not bat, bowl or dismiss anyone in the field. He did field for 66.5 overs and subsequently became England's oldest surviving Test cricketer before being summoned by the Great Scorer when eight days adrift of his 91st birthday.

 What value of English banknote featured a cricket match? **Anthony Robinson, London**

BEARDERS' ANSWER: That was a £10 note (Series E) issued in 1992. It depicted Charles Dickens and a scene from All-Muggleton's home match against Dingley Dell in chapter seven of his first novel, *The Pickwick Papers*.

Who made the first stumping in the history of Test matches? **Bilal, Canada**

BEARDERS' ANSWER: J.M. ('Jack') Blackham made the first stumping in Test cricket when he dismissed Alfred Shaw off the bowling of Tom Kendall in England's second innings of the inaugural Test, at Melbourne on 19 March 1877. Blackham's 35 caps included Australia's first 17 Tests and he captained his country eight times.

In 1997, I scored a 102 not out in a League match against Hatherleigh, batting at No. 11. Is this a record? How many centuries have been scored by people batting at No. 11? **Martin Heslip, UK**

BEARDERS' ANSWER: I suspect that there are many instances of No. 11 batsmen scoring hundreds in minor cricket. It has never been achieved in Tests or limited-overs internationals, the highest scores being 75 and 43 respectively.

There have been ten instances in First-Class cricket, the highest of which is 163 by T.P.B. (Peter) Smith for Essex v Derbyshire at Chesterfield in 1947.

Was there any occasion in a Test match between England and Australia when Lillee was caught in the gully by Willey off Dilley? **Lionel Rajapakse, Sri Lanka**

BEARDERS' ANSWER: There was indeed, and I was fortunate enough to be scoring for *TMS* at the WACA in Perth when it happened at 4.08pm on 18 December 1979, the fourth day of the first Anglo-Australian Test since the Packer schism. Dennis Lillee had scored 19 off his previous 104 balls in 135 minutes when he fended a short delivery from Graham Dilley to Peter Willey at close gully.

Earlier in this match Lillee had caused a ten-minute stoppage by using a bat made of aluminium.

Q When was a Test match last played on a matting pitch? Suggestions included Pakistan or the West Indies during the mid 1950s. **Chris Rawson, UK**

BEARDERS' ANSWER: Pakistan did indeed stage the last Tests to be played on matting, the final one being at Karachi's National Stadium on 4–9 December 1959. On the fourth day, Dwight D. Eisenhower became the first President of the United States of America to attend a Test match. He was rewarded with the second-slowest day's play in Test history, Pakistan scoring 104 for 5.

The last jute matting pitch to stage Test cricket in any other country was at Queen's Park Oval, Port-of-Spain, Trinidad in March 1954 when West Indies (681-8 dec and 212-4 dec) and England (537 and 98-3) averaged 64 runs per wicket in a six-day run fest.

How many English-born players have represented Australia? **Richard Dawson, UK**

BEARDERS' ANSWER: Nine Australian Test cricketers have been born in England:

C. Bannerman (Woolwich)
H. Carter (Halifax)
W.H. Cooper (Maidstone)
A.R. Dell (Lymington)
J.R. Hodges (London)
T.K. Kendall (Bedford)
P.S. McDonnell (London)
W.E. Midwinter (St Briavels, Glos)
H.A. Musgrove (Surbiton, Surrey)

In addition, A.A. Jackson was born in Scotland, and T.J.D. Kelly was born in Ireland.

Why are 'Test' matches so named? Why the word 'Test'? **Simon, USA**

BEARDERS' ANSWER: The phrase 'Test match' was coined in 1861–1862 during the very first cricket tour of Australia. The contests between H.H. Stephenson's

English team and each of the Australian colonies were described as 'Test matches'.

Why 'Test'? Probably because they provided the first opportunity to test the relative skills of English and Australian cricketers. They could easily have been described as 'Trials'.

Q Do you have any ideas about when eight-ball overs were played, what countries played eight-ball overs and when and why did they finish playing them? **Nigel Witter, Australia**

BEARDERS' ANSWER: The eight-ball over was first used in California. An Australian team visiting there took the concept home and it was introduced to their First-Class cricket in 1918–1919 when it resumed after the First World War. Australia were the first to introduce it at Test level (1924–1925). England began a two-year experiment with eight-ball overs in 1939, but the Second World War prevented any First-Class matches being played in 1940. Eight-ball overs were last used in 1978–1979 (by Australia and New Zealand).

A full list by countries of the number of balls to an over in Test cricket is given in each volume of my *Wisden Book of Test Cricket*.

Q Has anyone made a century made up only of singles? If not, who has made a ton without scoring any boundaries? **Nico Fell, UK**

BEARDERS' ANSWER: No! There are two recorded instances of hundreds without boundaries:

A. Hill (103) Orange Free State v Griqualand West at Bloemfontein in 1976–1977.

P.A. Hibbert (100) Victoria v Indians at Melbourne in 1977–1978.

Q Has it ever happened that a wicket-keeper got rid of his gloves and started bowling a few overs? Is it even allowed? **Alexander, The Netherlands**

BEARDERS' ANSWER: It is most certainly allowed, and it has frequently happened at all levels of the game. There are two instances of wicket-keepers handing over their gauntlets and taking hat-tricks in First-Class matches. Probir Sen achieved this feat for Bengal against Orissa at Cuttack in 1954–1955, and A.C. (Alan) Smith emulated him for Warwickshire against Essex at Clacton in 1965.

The most famous instance in Test cricket occurred at the Oval in 1884 when Alfred Lyttelton took 4-19 for England against Australia, bowling lobs while still wearing his pads and with W.G. Grace deputising behind the stumps.

I heard recently that in 1982 the first incident of a substitute taking a wicket occurred. How did this come about? **Greg, UK**

BEARDERS' ANSWER: When Gladstone Small was called up by an injury-stricken England team for the Edgbaston Test against Pakistan on the second morning of Warwickshire's Championship match against Lancashire at Southport, the TCCB playing conditions permitted a full substitute to replace him. Thus, on 29 July 1982, David Brown became the first substitute to take a wicket in county cricket.

Last season Kevin Innes scored an undefeated 103 while substituting for James Kirtley for Sussex against Nottinghamshire at Horsham.

How often in Test cricket has a team won by a single run? **Greg, US**

BEARDERS' ANSWER: You certainly move around, Greg! The steps folk go to just to get two questions in the same Ask Bearders!

Only one Test match has been decided by a single run. Inappropriately, it occurred at the Adelaide Oval on Australia Day 1993 when West Indies were the victors and thus retained the Frank Worrell Trophy. Tim May and Craig McDermott had added 40 for the last wicket when the latter failed to evade a lifting ball from Courtney Walsh which just flicked his glove. It was a brave decision by Australian umpire Darrell Hair to give him out.

Q What are the world records for successive wins and losses of the toss by captains? **James, England**

BEARDERS' ANSWER: The record for consecutive toss losses by one country is 12 by England (1959–1960 in WI (5); 1960 v SA (5); 1961 v A (2)). The captains were P.B.H. May (3) and M.C. Cowdrey (9).

Curiously, the record for consecutive toss wins by one country is also 12 – by Australia (1998–1999 in Pak (2), v Eng (5) and in WI (4); 1999-2000 in SL (1)). The captains were M.A. Taylor (7) and S.R. Waugh (5).

Q How many instances are there in Test cricket of captains who won the toss and inserted the opposition, as Daniel Vettori did in the last Test, losing the match by an innings? **Peter Graham, Bexley, Kent**

BEARDERS' ANSWER: There has been a total of 486 instances of insertion by 144 captains [as at June 2008]. They have resulted in 176 wins, 145 losses and 165 draws.

New Zealand's defeat at Trent Bridge was the 27th to involve an innings margin. The full list by team (with captains) is: Australia 1 (K.J. Hughes); England 5 (A.E. Stoddart, L. Hutton, M.H. Denness, I.T. Botham, D.I. Gower); South Africa 1 (H.W. Taylor); West Indies 1 (B.C. Lara); New Zealand 3 (M.D. Crowe – 2, D.L. Vettori); India 1 (S.R. Tendulkar); Pakistan 3 (Javed Burki, Zaheer Abbas, Waqar Younis); Sri Lanka 5 (D.S. de Silva, A. Ranatunga, S.T. Jayasuriya, M.S. Atapattu, D.P.M.D. Jayawardena); Zimbabwe 4 (S.V. Carlisle, H.H. Streak – 2, T. Taibu); Bangladesh 3 (Khaled Masud – 2, Habibul Bashar).

 **What** is the highest number of ex-captains playing in a Test team? **Rajeev Kumar, UK**

BEARDERS' ANSWER: The answer could well be three. England had Michael Atherton, Mark Butcher and Alec Stewart when Nasser Hussain was captain in three of the 2001 Ashes Tests, plus Graham Thorpe (past) and Marcus Trescothick (future) captains in limited-overs internationals.

Q Has there ever been a Test card for a single innings that gave the names of every member of both teams, as all bowlers took a wicket and the non bowlers all took catches? **Alan Kirkup, England**

BEARDERS' ANSWER: I haven't spotted one, but I scored a county match at Leicester in 1967 where in Northamptonshire's first innings all ten wickets fell to catches by different Leicestershire fielders. Jack Birkenshaw was alone in not claiming one, but he took three wickets.

Q   Usman Afzaal is the first Notts player I can recall to be at the crease when England won a Test match. Who, if any, was the last? **Tim Smith, UK**

BEARDERS' ANSWER: You win the award for the most esoteric question I have received this summer, Tim, and the one which involved most research!

The answer is that the last Nottinghamshire player before Afzaal was R.T. (Tim) Robinson (in partnership with Robin Smith, who made the winning hit) against Sri Lanka at Lord's on 30 August 1988. The victory ended a record sequence of 18 Tests without a win.

Incidentally, Afzaal is only the second player with a 'z' in his name to represent England. The first was S.S. (Sandford) Schultz, who played his only Test in 1878–1879 and changed his name to Storey when German popularity began to wane.

Q I have heard it said that Ryan Sidebottom and his father Arnold are the tenth father and son pair to be capped for England. Can you help me finish my list of the other nine: Gunn; Hardstaff; Hutton; Hobbs; Cowdrey… and then I get stuck. **Richard Tyndall, UK**

BEARDERS' ANSWER: Omit Gunn and Hobbs! The full list is:

A.R. and M.A. Butcher; M.C. and C.S. Cowdrey; J. sen. and J. jun. Hardstaff; L. and R.A. Hutton; F.T. and F.G. Mann; J.H. and J.M. Parks; A. and R.J. Sidebottom; M.J. and A.J. Stewart; F.W. and M.W. Tate; C.L. and D.C.H. Townsend.

In addition, Dean Headley's father and grandfather played for West Indies while the senior Nawab of Pataudi, who represented England and India, produced the junior version who captained India.

Q Has anyone claimed a diamond duck (first ball of the match) on debut in a Test match? **Tom Williamson, England**

BEARDERS' ANSWER: S.J. (Jimmy) Cook – having waited two decades for an official Test cap and uniquely having played in all of South Africa's 19 matches against rebel sides. He edged a late outswinger to third slip off Kapil Dev's opening ball of the First Test between South Africa and India at Durban in November 1992 to become the first (and to date only) debutant to be dismissed by the first ball of a Test.

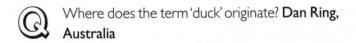 Who is the only England Test cricketer ever to have stood as a parliamentary candidate? **Baz Druker, England**

BEARDERS' ANSWER: Another trick question? There have been at least two.

F.S. Jackson (later the Rt Hon Sir Francis Stanley Jackson, GCSI, GCIE), was MP for the Howdenshire division of Yorkshire, 1915–1926. He also served as financial secretary to the War Office, chairman of the Unionist Party and Governor of Bengal.

E.R. (Ted) Dexter, current President of MCC, stood unsuccessfully as Conservative candidate for Cardiff SE in opposition to James Callaghan in 1964.

Where does the term 'duck' originate? **Dan Ring, Australia**

BEARDERS' ANSWER: It evolved from 'duck's egg', the shape of which bears a close resemblance to the figure '0'. Similarly, the term 'love' in tennis derives from l'oeuf ('the egg').

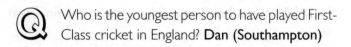

I recently read of a West Indian who is the only Test cricketer from any country to have been executed. Who was this man and what records (Test, not criminal) did he possess? **Matt Richards**

BEARDERS' ANSWER: Your man was Leslie George Hylton, a Jamaican fast bowler who was hanged in Spanish Town on 17 May 1955 for the murder of his wife. He played in six Tests (1934–1935 to 1939, in which year he toured England), achieving a best analysis of 4 for 27 and a highest score of 19. In 40 First-Class matches he took 120 wickets at 25.62 (best analysis 5 for 24) and scored 843 runs at 18.73 (highest score 80).

Who is the youngest person to have played First-Class cricket in England? **Dan (Southampton)**

BEARDERS' ANSWER: Charles Robertson Young was 15 years, 131 days old when he played for Hampshire against Kent at Gravesend on 13 June 1867. Born in Indiaat Dharwar near Bombay, the son of an assistant superintendent revenue surveyor for Southern Marathee County, his date of birth has been confirmed as 2 February 1852 at the India Office.

Q Does Uda Walawwe Mahim Bandaralage Chanaka Asanka Welegedara now have the longest name of anyone to have played Test cricket? **Russell Irwin**

BEARDERS' ANSWER: He doesn't have the longest surname, but he is the first Test cricketer to boast six initials.

Q I was recently amusingly told that Geraint Jones went his entire Test career without getting a duck, until succumbing to a pair in his last appearance. Is this accurate? **BarrellChestedDave**

BEARDERS' ANSWER: Your Jones statement is correct; he batted 51 times before bagging a pair in his final two innings.

Q How many Test captains have there ever been [as at November 2005]? I guess England has had the most? Which team has had the most in terms of Captains/Matches? **Rajiv Radhakrishnan, UK**

BEARDERS' ANSWER: There have been 273 Test captains and, yes, England has appointed the most (75), but they have also played more Tests (839) than any other team. Bangladesh captains average only 10.0 Tests apiece and South Africa's 10.01 each. Sri Lanka has the lowest turnover rate with 17.0 Tests per skipper, with Australia second on 15.9. The totals are (team's total Tests in brackets): Australia 42 (670), Bangladesh 4 (40), England 75 (839), India 28 (387), New Zealand 25 (324), Pakistan 25 (312), South Africa 30 (303), Sri Lanka 9 (153), West Indies 28 (423), and Zimbabwe 7 (83).

Q Can you recall any Test series of five or more matches where a side has used just 11 players throughout? **Peter Popper, UK**

BEARDERS' ANSWER: There have been only three five-Test rubbers in which a team has been unchanged:

ENGLAND v Australia in Australia, 1884–1885;
SOUTH AFRICA v England in South Africa, 1905–1906;
WEST INDIES v Australia in West Indies, 1990–1991.

Q A few years ago, there was an experiment during one-day internationals where both innings were split into two sections of 25, with each team taking it in turns to complete 25 overs before returning to field.

How many games were played and why have they stopped with this idea? **J, England (brum)**

BEARDERS' ANSWER: There has never been such an experiment in limited-overs internationals but England were involved in such shenanigans when they played a 'quartered' day/night match against Western Australia in Perth on 27 October 1994.

Each team faced 25 overs in daylight and then resumed for another 25 overs under floodlights. This was the first match between First-Class teams to be played in such a format. Critics and players were divided in their reactions to this concept and I have no record of it ever being repeated.

Q How many England cricketers have had the letter X in their surname? **Stephen Robinson, Scarborough**

BEARDERS' ANSWER: Five: Alex COXON, Ted DEXTER, Neville KNOX, Martyn MOXON and Roger PRIDEAUX.

At Close of Play

Bearders' Last Blog

This is Bearders' last BBC blog, posted at thirteen minutes past one on Monday 12 January 2009 (you can almost hear him saying 'I assume you mean thirteen minutes past one pm'). It was posted shortly before he contracted legionnaires' disease while with the Lords Taverners in Dubai. Black humour was something of a theme in his Ask Bearders blogs and this one was no exception, mentioning some bizarre and unusual ways in which cricketers were – as he often put it – 'summoned to the Great Scorer'.

His final entry was in response to a juicy lob from a Dubai listener concerning England Test hundreds on tour. The answer was duly despatched but not before Bearders, ever ready to engage with his audience, had extended a friendly invitation to meet up. 'I hope to see you when I am over there,' he told his correspondent.

Ask Bearders #185

Post categories: Ask Bearders
Bill Frindall | 13:13 GMT, Monday, 12 January 2009

Welcome to Ask Bearders, where *Test Match Special* statistician Bill 'The Bearded Wonder' Frindall answers your questions on all things cricket.

Below are Bill's responses to some of your questions posed at the end of his last column and if you have a question for Bill, leave it at the end of this blog entry. Please do include your country of residence – Bill loves to hear where all his correspondents are posting from.

Bill isn't able to answer all of your questions, however. BBC Sport staff will choose a selection of them and send them to Bearders for him to answer.

Q I've been doing my own research into this but have hit a bit of a brick wall. I'm trying to compile a list of players who have taken a Test wicket, made a Test stumping and scored a Test hundred, obviously not necessarily in the same match. So far, I have Mark Boucher, A.B. de Villiers and Javed Miandad, but I'd expect to find a couple more. Could you help at all on this? **Mike (Liverpool)**

BEARDERS' ANSWER: Intriguingly no Australian and only one Englishman has qualified for this eclectic club which has a dozen members:

England – J.M. Parks (2 hundreds, 1 wicket, 11

stumpings); South Africa – M.V. Boucher (5, 1, 2), A.B. de Villiers (7, 2, 1); West Indies – R.J. Christiani (1, 3, 2), C.L. Walcott (15, 11, 11); New Zealand – J.R. Reid (6, 85, 1); India – S.M.H. Kirmani (2, 1, 38), V.L. Manjrekar (7, 1, 2); Pakistan – Aamer Malik (2, 1, 1), Javed Miandad (23, 17, 1), Taslim Arif (1, 1, 3); Zimbabwe – Tatenda Taibu (1, 1, 4). Clyde Walcott is alone in reaching double figures in all three categories.

Q Has anybody apart from Andrew Strauss been on the losing side despite scoring a century in both innings of a Test match? **Jez229**

BEARDERS' ANSWER: Strauss is the eighth batsman to join this list:

H. Sutcliffe 176 127 E v A Melbourne Jan 1925
G.A. Headley 106 107 WI v E Lord's Jun 1939
V.S. Hazare 116 145 I v A Adelaide Jan 1948
C.L. Walcott 155 110 WI v A Kingston Jun 1955
S.M. Gavaskar 111 137 I v P Karachi Nov 1978
A. Flower 142 199* Z v SA Harare Sep 2001
B.C. Lara 221 130 WI v SL Colombo Nov 2001
A.J. Strauss 123 108 E v I Madras Dec 2008

Q In Tests, what is the highest first innings total posted by a team batting first, only to go on to lose the match? **devonFRATTONiser**

BEARDERS' ANSWER: Australia's 586 all out at Sydney in December 1894 remains the highest losing total for the opening innings of a Test match. England replied with 325 and, following on, scored 437 before the left-arm spin of Bobby Peel (6-67) and Johnny Briggs (3-25) snatched victory by ten runs on a 'sticky' pitch. The first Test to involve a sixth playing day, it was also the first to be won by a team following on. Spare a thought for George Giffen, Australia's champion all-rounder, who contributed 202 runs and eight wickets to a losing cause.

Q Greetings from the US where we have one real turf wicket! I was wondering (surprisingly hard to find) how many sides have won a Test series in Australia. If you subtract West Indies (1970–2000) and England (1877–1900), it must be only a handful? **CowCornerCathedral**

BEARDERS' ANSWER: In fact it is two handfuls! Discounting the seasons you list, England have won eight series in Australia (1903–1904, 1911–1912, 1928–1929, 1932–1933, 1954–1955, 1970–1971, 1978–1979, 1986–1987), New Zealand one (1985–1986) and now

South Africa one (2008–2009).

Presumably your turf wicket is on the Woodley Complex in Los Angeles, where I had the privilege of playing for the MCC in 1991. Only last week I received an invitation from the Corinthians Cricket Club to speak at their 75th Anniversary Dinner in October and play for the Occasionals at Woodley the following day. I will look out for you at Cow Corner!

Q I have a question about Greek Cricketers. Now I know that ex-Aussie fast bowler Jason Gillespie is half Greek and Hampshire's South African keeper, Nic Pothas, is also of Greek descent – but are these the only 'Greeks' to have played international cricket? By the way, we have a new ground in Athens which, fingers crossed, will herald the rise of the Minotaurs on the world cricket scene. **ElGrecoAthens**

BEARDERS' ANSWER: No Test cricketer was actually born in Greece. Zenophon Constantine Balaskas, a thickset leg-spinner and a lower-order batsman skilled enough to score two First-Class double centuries, had Greek parents. Born in Johannesburg in 1910 and known as 'Bally' or 'Saxophone', he appeared for no fewer than five First-Class provincial teams as well as in nine Tests. Notably, at Lord's in 1935, he contributed nine wickets to South Africa's first victory in England.

One Test cricketer, L.J. (Leonard) Moon, died

in Greece. His 96 First-Class matches, mainly for Cambridge University and Middlesex, included four Tests for England in South Africa in 1905–1906. An aggressive opening batsman who scored 138 against the 1899 Australians, he could also keep wicket. As a 2nd Lieutenant with the Devon Regiment during the First World War, he died of wounds near Karasouli, Salonica, in 1916.

Congratulations on acquiring your new ground in Athens. As Patron of their Cricket Board, I will advise Germany to tour there.

Q How many times has a Test side scored 400+ runs and lost all 10 wickets in one day? I think it happened in 2005 between England and Australia. **sleepingkerrps**

BEARDERS' ANSWER: Your instance was in that epic match at Edgbaston when Ricky Ponting ignored the loss of key bowler Glenn McGrath through a freak training accident shortly before the start, put England in and bowled them out for 407 in 79.2 overs just before stumps. England eventually scraped to victory by two runs – the narrowest runs margin in Ashes Tests. I have found five other instances (match day in brackets):

South Africa 451 (2nd) v New Zealand Christchurch 1931–1932

Australia 450 (1st) v South Africa Johannesburg 1921–1922
Australia 448 (1st) v South Africa Manchester 1912
England 428 (1st) v South Africa Lord's 1907
Australia 407 (1st) v England Leeds 1921

Q I notice that you often refer to the method or location of death of cricketers. Is this an interest? What is the most unusual method of death for a First-Class cricketer? **sirianblog**

BEARDERS' ANSWER: When I compiled my Index of Test Cricketers for *The Wisden Book of Test Cricket* series, I included their places of birth and, where appropriate, death. In researching my 'England Test Cricketers', I found that fate had dealt a surprising number with bizarre and unusual ends. My favourites include: crushed by a crane loading sugar aboard the SS *Muriel* (Charlie Absolom); in a mud hut after falling off a cart and being interred in a coffin made from whisky cases (Monty Bowden); as he was putting on his boots to go to work (Johnny Tyldesley); from pneumonia contracted while watching Yorkshire play at Sheffield (George Ulyett); from septicaemia after falling on a dance floor ('Dodger' Whysall).

Q I think England win more Tests when Hoggard plays and lose more Tests when Anderson plays. How many of Hoggard's 67 Tests have England won? How many of Anderson's 31 Tests have England lost? **COMMONSENSECRICKET**

BEARDERS' ANSWER: Only because Matthew Hoggard has played more than double the number of Tests enjoyed by James Anderson your statement is basically correct! Expressed as a percentage the difference is a mere 1.11%. England have won 31 (46.27%), lost 18 and drawn 18 of Hoggard's 67 Tests. Anderson's 31 appearances have resulted in 14 wins (45.16%), 11 defeats and six draws. Their nine joint appearances began with a sequence of six wins but ended with three defeats.

Q Bangladesh recently scored 413 in the fourth innings in their attempt to score 521 to beat Sri Lanka. Aside from the fact that this shows they can make a big score, what is the highest ever fourth-innings score in Test and First-Class cricket? **aarongeordie**

BEARDERS' ANSWER: The record fourth-innings score in all First-Class matches is the 654-5 amassed by England in the timeless Test at Durban in March 1939. Beginning on the day I was born, it was abandoned as a draw 11 days later (when rain ended play at tea with England just 42 runs short of victory), because the tourists had to begin a two-day train journey to catch their ship in Cape Town.

(Q) During a recent Australia v South Africa Test match, I noticed that four leg-byes were scored in an over, yet no other runs. When they showed the bowling stats later, that over was considered a maiden. Why don't leg-byes count towards a bowler's stats? **copperspa**

BEARDERS' ANSWER: Simply because neither byes nor leg-byes result from bowling errors, whereas no-balls and wides do. Not until 1983–1984 were penalties and runs scored off no-balls and wides debited to a bowler's analysis. Before that season, maiden overs could include no-balls and wides.

(Q) Recently you have been referring to ODIs as 'internationals', where you used to call them LOIs. Is there any reason for this? Do you include Twenty20 games in this classification? **Aaron (Newcastle upon Tyne)**

BEARDERS' ANSWER: I have always referred to them by the correct nomenclature of Limited-Overs Internationals. That was their original title and it was the only one used when, in the mid-1980s, the then ICC Secretary Jack Bailey commissioned me to compile a list of all such internationals commencing with their accidental conception at Melbourne in January 1971. They are not 'One-Day Internationals' because a substantial number have involved more than a single day's play. In these blogs, I use the term 'internationals' in deference to BBC Online's instruction to avoid the abbreviation 'LOI'. Twenty-over matches are Very Limited-Overs Internationals. Their statistics are a separate entity and do not qualify for inclusion in List A records.

Q Which England players have scored a hundred in both innings of a Test on tour apart from Strauss and Compton in Adelaide in 1947? **Paul Hawkins (Dubai)**

BEARDERS' ANSWER: Thank you for your question, 'Hawkeye'. I hope to see you when I am over there with the Lord's Taverners later this week.

Five others have scored hundreds in both innings for England overseas: C.A.G. 'Jack' Russell (Durban 1922–1923); Herbert Sutcliffe (Melbourne 1924–1925); Wally Hammond (Adelaide 1928–1929); Eddie Paynter (Johannesburg 1938–1939); and Alec Stewart (Bridgetown 1993–1994).

***

At the end of this final blog, Bill's correspondents continued to post questions and discussion points right through January 2009, unaware that he was fighting for his life. The last topic of Ask Bearders #185 – post No. 167 – was an appropriately arcane debate (which Bearders would surely have relished) started by club player tigermilkboy. He explained how, in going for a close catch, he managed to knock the ball towards the batsman. The batsman jabbed at the ball (which had still not touched the ground) hitting it back to tigermilkboy, who gratefully caught it. The batsman walked but tigermilkboy clearly felt guilty, believing 'dead ball' should have been called. According to other blog contributors, quoting Laws 32 and 34, he needn't have worried. It was a fair catch. The last two posts drop 3 hours and 55 minutes later as news of Bill's death begins to filter through to a stunned cricketing world:

- 171. At 3:23pm on 30 Jan 2009, Jordan D wrote:
  Just seen the breaking news. RIP Bill.

- 172. At 3:23pm on 30 Jan 2009, Princessbonzai wrote:
  How awful. Test Match cricket just won't be the same without him. How can you replace someone like that?

It's one question Bearders' thousands of devotees could have answered without his help.
  You can't.

Index of People